ANGER

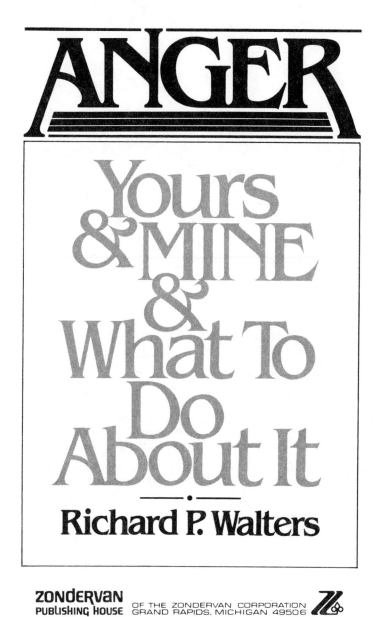

ANGER

Yours & MINE & What To Do About It

Richard P. Walters

ZONDERVAN
PUBLISHING HOUSE OF THE ZONDERVAN CORPORATION
GRAND RAPIDS, MICHIGAN 49506

Library of Congress Cataloging in Publication Data
Walters, Richard P., 1935-
    Anger—yours and mine and what to do about it.

    1. Anger—moral and religious aspects.   I. Title.
BV4627.A5W34   248.8'6   81-12997
ISBN 0-310-42601-4   AACR2

Contents

Preface

This is an overview of anger for the layperson. I have attempted to explain what anger is, where it comes from, and what to do with it. I have wanted, first, for everything stated here to be consistent with the Bible, and second, for it to be useful in your life.

Because anger is a secondary emotion, one that follows other events and feelings, this book cannot give you the complete information that you might need in order to resolve specific conflicts in your own life. But it describes principles and will help you identify sources and causes of conflict, even though it cannot treat those fully. I have seen these principles and methods work dramatically in the lives of many persons. I urge you to get the assistance of a competent professional counselor for help with major or long-lasting problems.

Chapter 3 and most of chapter 12 were written by Miriam McNair Engler. It has been particularly helpful to have the benefit of her seminary and counseling training and clinical experience included in this book. Rachel Walters contributed extensive, valuable help in preliminary research.

A filmstrip compatible with principles within this book is available from Christian Helpers, Inc., 5500 Waterbury Place S.E., Kentwood, MI 49508.

The illustrative stories are all based on fact, but the names and situations have been altered and intermingled so that none of the characters portrayed is an actual person. The incidents are less extreme than those seen routinely in counseling practice, and they represent events common to the lives of many Christian persons.

My only aspiration for the book is that it will help you to be more alive in your relationship to God and His kingdom. Nothing is more important.

1

Let's Get Indignant!

"My mother says if I'd only get straightened out spiritually, everything would be okay. But what do I want with their religion, for all the good it does them? Look at this," she said, pointing to her legs. They were a mass of ugly bruises from ankles to knees. "And," she added, "you're not even seeing half of what my mother did to me."

"When did she do that?" I asked.

"Oh, that happened on the night I was arrested for speeding," she said.

I was talking with Debby, a high-school junior, and it took a while to get the whole story. I found out that the parents believe that Debby is demon-possessed. They had invited a few friends over and, insisting on Debby's participation, had prayed for exorcism. After the guests went home and her parents had gone to bed, Debby found a bottle of wine, drank half of it, and "borrowed" the family car. Within an hour she was arrested for exceeding the speed limit and driving without a license. Her parents were angry when they picked her up at the police station; her mother expressed this by kicking and beating Debby when they got home.

The mother later told me, "The family could get along if it weren't for Debby's spiritual problems." She honestly believed that. She blindly, ignorantly, and honestly believed this because, as she said, "We're living the way we are supposed to."

Debby's father tried to be a strong leader in his family. Unfortunately, he believed physical force was the way to assert his God-given authority.

Anger moves through families with more predictability than red hair. The hostility was passed from husband to wife and from wife to daughter. Debby needed to eat, so she kept coming home and she kept quiet. She'd be punished if she "rebelled against the authority of the home," her father yelled. The pressure grew. It seemed to Debby that nothing she did would please her parents and all she got for her efforts were bruises. But what could she do? The pressure continued to grow.

Then Debby met a boy who cared about her and understood how she felt. He understood, because his home had been worse than hers, and that understanding meant enough to Debby. It wasn't important to her that he believed he was homosexual, that he didn't own a toothbrush, or that he hadn't worked in the three months since he'd been fired for incompetence from a menial job. She didn't care about any of that, because he cared for her more than her parents did. Being cared about was something new and different to Debby, and she thought it was wonderful.

Let's Get Indignant!

Debby's father didn't think it was so wonderful. One night when her boyfriend arrived, Debby's father looked at him leaning against the wall with his shirttail hanging out, his fly unzipped, and a transistor radio pressed against his ear. Her father came unglued. "Get out of here, you scruffy punk!" he yelled, and he shoved Debby's friend backward through the screen door.

The boy moved away, and things were very quiet in the household. Father was pleased. It soon became even quieter, however, when Debby took a Greyhound bus to join her boyfriend and to set up house with the only person she'd ever known who cared about her. Her mother said, "See—I knew she'd make a mess of things!"

Rage—rotten, insane, senseless, sinful, criminal behavior—bombarded bewildered Debby. She resented it and hated her parents, but hated herself even more because she felt so worthless. She felt so unloved that five times she tried to kill herself, hoping her mom and dad would take an interest in her. Her mother said, "I don't care if she dies, after all the trouble she's caused me."

Debby's parents had mastered the deadly art of rage and were getting away with it. Her father had killed his conscience with perverse distortions of Christianity and had convinced his family to tolerate his criminal behavior. Her mother was adept at projecting the parental sins onto Debby and matching father's physical punishment blow for blow. They had perfected deception, for there probably was not a member of their large church who would have believed a word of what you've just read about Debby's parents. About Debby, yes; about her parents, never!

11

This was a sick family driving each other to hell's door in the presence of a church family that smugly condemned Debby's frantic, desperate clutching after the "life abundant" that Christ had come to bring her. Doesn't this arouse indignation in you?

The Proper Reaction

Indignation is the proper reaction to injustice if it energizes our physical and emotional systems to oppose evil, to right the wrongs that have been done to those we care about, and to work hard for social changes that will spare others from abuse and suffering. Feelings of anger can spring out of a Christian's sensitivity to human welfare. While rage and resentment are aggressive, seeking to destroy their target, indignation seeks to mobilize the forces of good to challenge and defeat the forces of destruction and oppression. Indignation is the opposite of complacent acceptance of evil conditions. My response to an incident that happened many years ago illustrates indignation.

One of my close friends had personal and family problems that seemed overwhelming. Seeking help, he went to a counseling center operated by a large church in his city. At the beginning of his first appointment the counselor said, "You wouldn't believe the situation of that lady just in here! What problems! But I gave her a lot of help!" He began describing the problems and his response to them with the spotlight on the thought "Look at what a terrific counselor I am! Aren't I Great!"

My friend looked that self-centered counselor in the eye and said, "It's obvious that you are more interested in talking about yourself than in listening to me," and walked out. It was his last contact with organized

Christianity in seven years. It was seven years of living hell for him, tottering on the brink of suicide, and seven years of pain and uncertainty for his family.

Using Anger Righteously

My friend survived, and through God's faithful care, normal family life was restored. But when I think of the incompetence and indifference of the counselor who bungled an opportunity to help my friend, I become angry. Why? Because a Christian, in a position to help others, couldn't see beyond the illusion of his own self-importance. He failed without having tried. When I recall that counselor's inexcusable professional failure, I am angry because the seven years of my friend's suffering might have been prevented. That fresh sense of anger, properly channeled and committed to God's service can help me to stay determined to put the other person first when I counsel.

Rage and resentment are destructive expressions of anger; indignation is a constructive loving expression. When we feel angry, for whatever reasons, it is the common experience of all persons, Christians and nonbelievers alike, to move toward destructive expressions unless there is a willful decision to think, act, and feel constructively. If we choose, there are constructive paths to follow in coping with the feelings of anger and resolving the root causes.

God wants us to be stirred to action. Indignation is one of the energizing, activating mechanisms God has given us as a tool. We are God's body on earth. Our indignation is given to us to fire up our engines and to run our bodies for God's service.

We must be a voice to protest evil where we live, to

say, "That's not fair!" and "You may not do that!" We are a voice to ask the unanswerable, to love the unforgiving, and to forgive the unkind. We are to mobilize those around us to action, to be voices to prod others to awareness of needs, to inflame their hearts with passion for service.

We must be arms to pull down the facades of hypocrisy, to throw out impersonal, programmed churchianity, to sweep out the clutter of meaningless form, and to make room for a powerful renewal of an authentic living personal Christianity.

We must be legs to kick out the props of self-serving politics from leaders who speak empty words instead of proclaiming the glory of God's Word to a wisdom-starved generation.

We must have a strong back to shovel out the decaying remains of Pharisaisms and to till the ground for a new growth of wholesome, lifegiving spiritual food for a hungry world.

We must live lives that illustrate God's compassionate response to the wretchedness of the human condition and lives that celebrate God's eternal conquest of sin.

There is an image more beautiful than any image on earth, an image so beautiful that it cannot be captured on canvas or film or case in precious metal. It is the image of one person loving God enough to serve others totally, with complete energy, emotion, mind, and devotion, hurling oneself fully and passionately against the enemy Sin.

Such giving away of our selfish interests usually happens only after we have experienced indignation at the deadly path of sin, an indignation that approaches as closely as possible the intensity of God's own revulsion toward sin.

We should have this kind of indignation. We should seek this intensity of indignation. How much do you have? Please pray for more.

2

But Don't Stay Angry

The three expressions of anger—rage, resentment, and indignation—are vigorous expressions that combine emotion, physical activation, cognition, and behavior. In other words, when we are caught up in any one of these expressions, we are totally involved. For that reason, each has great potential for good or evil. For the most part, Christians don't engage in rage—which is violent, uncontrolled anger. Its wrongness is too visible. However, we would be better off with rage than with resentment, which is a repressed feeling of anger that smolders and seeks revenge, for we can be forced by societal pressures to resolve our rage. The common pattern among Christians is to create resentment by denying the existence of angry feelings and pushing them down inside. This pattern inevitably leads to tension and a subtle but concrete attack on others. Anger generates much physical energy, which resentment turns against one's own body. This is energy that should be used to correct basic causes of anger.

Rage seeks to do wrong, resentment seeks to hide wrong, indignation seeks to correct wrongs.

Rage and resentment seek to destroy people, indignation seeks to destroy evil.

Rage and resentment seek vengeance, indignation seeks justice.

Rage is guided by selfishness, resentment is guided by cowardice, indignation is guided by mercy.

Rage uses open warfare, resentment is a guerrilla fighter, indignation is an honest and fearless and forceful defender of truth.

Rage defends itself, resentment defends the status quo, indignation defends the other person.

Rage and resentment are forbidden by the Bible, indignation is required.

Recognizing the Differences

Among Christians there is a fear of rage, a surplus of resentment, and a shortage of indignation. We need to learn to recognize each, to protect ourselves from wrong, and to become strong enough to be forcefully and lovingly indignant in God's service. We can learn to recognize the three forms of anger by their qualities.

In chapter 1 we read an example of intense rage between people, the kind that should spark indignation in any sensitive person. Let's examine another story to see if it is similar to anything in our own experience.

Ralph was driving home through heavy traffic. Stop and go, stop and go. "After everything that has gone wrong today, I don't deserve to be stuck in this miserable city traffic," he thought irritably. He stopped again. His foot, jammed against the brake pedal, was aching. His fingers were clenched around the steering wheel. His neck was stiff with tension.

At home Sally had dinner on the stove and was ready to serve. She looked impatiently at the clock and saw that it was almost time for Ralph to arrive. Happily she thought that these several years of marriage had been the best years of her life. She smiled to herself, satisfied that Ralph's favorite foods were prepared and that he soon would be home.

Meanwhile, Ralph was trapped in a traffic snarl. As his irritation grew, he stared sullenly at the high prices posted in a gas station and wondered how much gas was being wasted while his car's engine was idling in the traffic jam. He searched the glove compartment for antacid tablets. His teeth were clenched, but he wasn't aware of it.

When Sally noticed that Ralph was now fifteen minutes late, she put their dinner back in the oven. Sighing with disappointment, because the meal was no longer fresh and hot, she recalled darkly that Ralph had been thirty minutes late the night before and that he had phoned only an hour ago to say he would be home on time tonight.

Ralph rolled into the driveway thirty minutes late and entered the house brusquely, slamming the door behind him. Sally met him cheerfully saying, "I have your favorite dinner ready. It'll take just a minute to put it on the table."

Ralph replied, "Never saw the traffic so lousy. It gets worse and worse! With the cost of driving, you'd think people would have enough sense to take the bus!" He stalked into the living room and sat in his favorite chair. Sally was busy in the kitchen. After five minutes she called, "Dinner is ready." There was no response from Ralph.

Sally arranged a few items on the table, noticing that the tossed salad was going limp and the mashed potatoes were drying out. She went into the living room, where Ralph sat reading the newspaper, and touched the top of the paper, saying softly, "Dinner is ready."

Ralph jumped up, wadding the newspaper and throwing it to the floor. "Get off my back, Sally! I just got home!" He kicked the newspaper out of the way and walked quickly to the dining area. "Oh, I'm sorry I yelled!" he said. "It was just a hard day at work, and then the lousy traffic got on my nerves! The meal looks good—let's eat!"

As Ralph said grace, Sally fought the impulse to ask him just who he thought he was to talk to God when the echoes of his angry yelling had scarcely died away. She fought the impulse to tell him how sick she was of his being late and coming in complaining. And she wanted to cry—to grieve aloud over the ruined dinner. But she wouldn't let herself do any of these, so there was nothing left but her silence and Ralph's comments about his rotten day at work.

That night, trying to go to sleep, Sally pictured herself shoving a bowl of cold mashed potatoes into Ralph's face. She would have laughed out loud had it not been for another thought, and a stab of sorrow, for the pleasant dinner for two that might have been. She wept silently.

"I'm sorry," Ralph said gently in the darkness. "Are you asleep?" Sally pretended she was.

Ralph was home for supper on time the next night, but the mashed potatoes were cold.

Anger is an emotional response to circumstances. It is a feeling, but one with strong ties to our thinking and with clear connections to our physical systems, so that we often use the word *anger* to refer to both the behavior and the feeling. We can see the two destructive expressions of the feeling of anger in the story about Ralph and Sally.

Rage is what Ralph displayed in throwing and kicking the paper. It is the violent, explosive, outward manifestation of anger. It is the opposite of peace.

Resentment is what Sally displayed when she ignored Ralph, pretending to be asleep and serving cold potatoes. It is the continuing, smoldering manifestation of anger, suppressed inside except when it sneaks out to seek revenge. It is the opposite of joy.

Righteous indignation, however, is a legitimate expression of love. This is anger expressed in a positive form. Anger is not only a killer; it can also be a lover.

Unfortunately, anger is often a killer. People will be murdered today because of someone's anger. Others, including many Christians, will die from physical ailments resulting from or aggravated by poor management of their angry feelings. Today many people will die in anger-related auto accidents, while others will carry out the angriest act of all—suicide. Continually, countless relationships die little by little as resentment gnaws away at the foundations of love and trust. Anger is a devastating force, and its consequences should sicken us. Anger-related destruction of the human life and spirit is an incredible national disaster. It is a personal tragedy in the lives of millions.

But Don't Stay Angry

The Basic Answer

The problem is great, yet the basic answer is simple. Anger must be displaced by the fruit of the Spirit. Peace and love can flow in and crowd out anger when Jesus is Lord of our lives.

In practical experience this transformation does not happen automatically. If it did, the control of anger would not be such a great emotional problem among Christians—perhaps the greatest we have. God's ways of helping us generally involve our conscious participation. We need to take time to learn about God's ways to help us control our responses to our emotions. We must learn to benefit from our emotions, to displace destructive responses with constructive responses, and to clear up the problems that result when we allow our emotions to lead us into destructive behavior.

The purpose of this book is to learn how we as Christians should handle our emotions specifically in regard to anger. We will learn to identify what causes anger in ourselves and to see why we must do something about our responses to anger. We will learn to seek God's will in learning how to control angry feelings, in placing our experiences with anger into perspective, and in dealing constructively with anger in another person. We will search God's Word for guidelines in learning these principles.

Some people are so fearful of the destructive potential in anger and so ashamed of their past performances that they deny ever having the feeling. Do you get angry, or do you only get annoyed or a bit irritated, bugged or ticked off? Do you admit to getting upset occasionally but hastily explain that it is always for a good reason? Well, these words describe different conditions of anger but they are so closely related that all of us may as well admit that, yes, we do get angry.

I was once in a doctor's waiting room when a married couple of about retirement age entered. The man presented himself to the receptionist for his appointment. She said that he was not scheduled that day, but he produced an appointment card from his wallet.

"Sure enough, you do have an appointment," the receptionist said. "I just didn't write it down in my book. I'm so sorry. We'll work you in as soon as we can." Then she said, "I imagine you're angry with me now."

At this the man's wife chimed in, "Oh no! He's not angry. Why, we've been married for forty-two years and he has never been angry!"

Do you believe that? I don't. They may have thought he had never been angry, but if he was never alive to feelings of anger, he probably was not alive to any other feelings either. Closing ourselves to unpleasant emotions simultaneously bars us from experiencing happy emotions. We must recognize that angry feelings can be okay, even though our responses may not be. People, especially in Christian circles, do not always agree that anger is acceptable. For many, anger is an emotion to be denied. We hear such statements as "A man is never worse company than when he flies into a rage and is beside himself." Maybe that's witty word play, but it is indefensible thinking.

Biblical Assumptions

Even though this is a common emotion and one mentioned frequently in the Bible, anger has often been misunderstood by Christians. It is essential that we get our assumptions in order and that these assumptions be biblical. Following are some basic, biblical assumptions about anger:

First, anger is an emotion and a feeling—not a behavior. Feelings generally are neither right or wrong in themselves, but they can lead either to right and constructive behavior or to wrong and destructive behavior. Behaviors and attitudes are right or wrong. To feel angry may be wrong, but frequently it is not. The destructive expressions of anger found in rage and resentment are wrong.

Second, anger is a universal emotional response and, therefore, Christians are not immune to becoming angry. Even Jesus felt anger. However, as Christians we can live with control over anger and we can learn practical aspects of getting along with ourselves and others.

Then, anger is usually a secondary emotion, meaning that there is an event or series of events that leads to an emotion such as hurt, envy, fear, loneliness, or frustration, with anger resulting later. Anger is often reflexive and unthinking, and it comes quickly; for all intents and purposes we do not have conscious control over its happening. We should not feel guilty about this.

Fourth, we do have a choice about how we behave after we become angry, and we are responsible for this behavior. An incident involving anger need not produce bad results; bad behavior can create additional problems for us and for others.

Next, the anger of others affects us for better or worse. We can learn to respond to angry persons with confidence, in love, and in ways that are helpful. It is our responsibility as Christians to do this.

Sixth, living a disciplined Christian life can reduce the number of occasions on which we inappropriately and unnecessarily feel angry.

These basic propositions, and more, are explained in greater detail in this book. We should begin the study of these concepts and helpful responses to anger by looking at what the Bible teaches on the subject.

3

Is Anger Right or Wrong?

Knowing what the Bible says about anger is essential to our understanding of its origin, expression, and prevention. Scripture speaks of anger frequently, showing it to be part of God's own nature, present in the interactions between God and His creatures, and occurring among His creatures.

If we were to compile all the words in the Old Testament meaning some form or degree of anger, we would discover 365 references to God's anger and 80 references to man's. The Hebrew word for "anger" that is used most frequently is *aph*, which translates literally as "nostril." This idea of snorting out anger is attributed 177 times to God and 45 times to man.

God's anger and man's anger have both similarities and differences in their nature. God's anger in the Old Testament is the response of His righteousness to

This chapter was written by Miriam McNair Engler.

man's sin and rebellion. The Bible views God's wrath as very proper. Because God is divine, His anger is a natural expression and reaction to man's unholiness and ungodliness. Yet, God's wrath is only one part of His character and is usually closely related to His love and compassion (see Jer. 10:24; Ezek. 23; Amos 3:2). God also describes Himself as being slow to anger (Ps. 103:8; Isa. 48; Jonah 4:2; Nah. 1:3). Thus, while His anger is viewed as a proper response to man's sin, God is also described as being slow to anger and loving and compassionate. The nature and direction of His anger are His righteous response against sin. The expression and limitations of His anger are His loving and patient character.

There are also Old Testament examples of godly yet angry men. God sometimes condemned their anger and sometimes approved of it.

Moses and Anger

Moses is one Old Testament saint who displayed both righteous and unrighteous anger. We can sympathize with Moses' anger in Exodus 32. He had just met with God—not only in spirit, but face to face. God, being faithful to His covenant promises, had given to Moses, for His people, the Ten Commandments as their guide. Then God told Moses about the Israelites' idol worship in their camp at the foot of Mount Sinai. As Moses brought to the people the tablets that God Himself had written, he heard the sound of singing and dancing in idol worship. "His anger burned," the Bible says, "and he threw the tablets out of his hands, breaking them to pieces at the foot of the mountain" (Exod. 32:19). Moses' anger was white hot against the people's ungodliness, yet there is no scriptural condemnation of Moses. It was very appropriate anger for Moses to have and express.

However, on another occasion, God did condemn an expression of anger by Moses. The people were thirsty and complaining, and Moses felt responsible: he felt the pressure of having to care for a multitude of people while not knowing how to go about it. In his frustration he acted impulsively rather than depending on God. (Num. 20:2–13). Moses' frustration became anger, not because God's righteousness was being violated, but because his own sense of responsibility was threatened. God rebuked Moses for this.

In both of these examples, we observe Moses feeling angry and allowing the feeling to influence his behavior—in one case appropriately, and in the other case inappropriately. God approves one expression and condemns the other. In neither case is the feeling of anger dealt with scripturally, but the behavior subsequent to the feeling is.

David is another Old Testament personality to whom the Bible attributes anger. As a young boy, David was righteously angry when he saw the Lord's army stopped in fear of the giant Goliath (1 Sam. 17). David knew that God's honor was not being upheld, and he wasn't going to allow that to continue. Although the Scriptures don't use the word *angry* here, this is a reasonable interpretation of David's emotional response to the tense political situation and the failure of his countrymen to depend on God. David allowed God to use his aroused emotions and direct them into useful behavior to defeat Goliath. God turned David's anger into blessing.

Yet another time, David "burned with anger" as he listened to the prophet Nathan's story of the rich man stealing from the poor (2 Sam. 12). David was stirred by the injustice in the story and declared that the ruthless rich man should be put to death. Then Nathan delivered the parable's punch line: "You, David, are the man!" On this occasion it may have been David's anger of indignation that made it possible for him to receive the accusations that God had sent Nathan to deliver.

So in Scripture it is clear both that anger exists in God's people and that God has definite responses to angry actions. But to this point in Scripture there is little comment regarding ways of dealing with anger.

Anger in the New Testament

To get a complete biblical view of anger we must examine what the New Testament says about it. The Greek language in the New Testament employs several words for "anger," but the two used most frequently are *thumos* and *orgē. Thumos* means a turbulent commotion, boiling agitation of feeling, sudden explosion; it is used approximately twenty times in the New Testament. It is equivalent to what we have defined as rage. *Orgē* is a long-lasting attitude that often continues to seek revenge; it appears forty-five times. It is comparable to the word *resentment* as it is used in this book. A third word, less common than the others, is *aganaktesis;* it is used five times and generally translated as "indignation," a form of anger without the implication of inappropriate behavior, which corresponds with the word *indignation* as it is used in this book. When we observe how all these words are used, we discover that, in the New Testament, anger is attributed to God about four times as often as it is attributed to man. We find approximately the same ratio in the Old Testament.

Because Jesus is the person of the Godhead dealt with most extensively in the New Testament, it is logical that most New Testament examples of divine anger are attributed to Him. There are times when Jesus' recorded words are clearly expressed in anger, even though anger may not be explicitly attributed to Him (in Matt. 23, for example). Yet, in throwing the money-changers out of the temple Jesus obviously both felt and acted angry. He also became angry with the Pharisees for their stubborn hearts (Mark 3:5) and indignant when children were kept away from Him (Mark 10:13–14). These are only a few of many New Testament examples of Jesus' righteous anger toward oppression, injustice, and unmet human needs. Jesus did not hesitate to express His angry feelings at all, yet we know He was righteous in everything He did.

Anger is also attributed to and commented on by various authors in the New Testament, the most notable being Paul. And although Peter didn't write about his own anger, we can see it expressed in his life. It is so easy to identify with Peter in his humanness throughout the Gospels. We might think especially of the churning emotions he must have felt in the Garden of Gethsemane when the soldiers came to take his Master: fear, confusion, anger. Peter acted immediately, cutting off the ear of the high priest's servant. Jesus responded to Peter's action—rebuking him for it—but He didn't address Peter's feelings of confusion and anger, only his actions. Jesus said, "Put your sword away" (John 18:10–11).

In contrast with Peter, Paul writes a great deal about

anger but we see only a few expressions of it in his recorded actions. Paul has more to say about anger than any other biblical writer. Drawing together all of Paul's many statements on anger, we can derive these principles:

1. Never take out vengeance (Rom. 12:19).
2. "In your anger, do not sin." Do not stay angry from one day to the next (Eph. 4:26–27);
3. "Get rid of all bitterness, rage and anger." Love each other in a forgiving way, just as in Christ God forgave us (Eph. 4:32);
4. Bear with one another charitably, in complete selflessness, gentleness, and patience (Eph. 4:2);
5. "Bear with each other" and forgive whatever grievances we have against others (Col. 3:13).

Additional examples of angry incidents in Scripture would serve to confirm the basic concepts that the biblical examples cited: Both God and man get angry. The way in which God expresses anger is always just; humans often express anger in ways that are wrong. God is described as being slow to anger and forgiving, and we are commanded to be the same.

A Dangerous Feeling

The feeling of anger is not wrong. But because the physiological activation that usually accompanies it can easily cloud our rational thinking and trigger our sinful inclinations, it is a very dangerous feeling. Thus it is wrong to treat it carelessly.

It is okay to feel anger. It is not okay to keep on feeling it. We cannot avoid feeling angry, but we are commanded to deal with it properly.

The feeling of anger, if not handled properly, seeks

expression in two destructive ways that can be roughly described as (1) rage—blowing up, and (2) resentment —stuffing it within. These are wrong expressions of anger.

A proper response to the effects of evil in the world is righteous indignation. The emotional and physiological components of this response may be identical to the emotional and physiological response of rage, but the cognitive and behavioral expressions are different. Indignation is unwilling to sit quietly by, watching the trampling of human dignity without raising the cry for justice and mercy and acting on it forcefully, as Christ did in driving the moneychangers from the temple.

God alone has the right to punish sin and to wreak vengeance. People never have that right; instead, we must always impose the limit of love on our expression of anger. We are frequently commanded to build up the body, love our brothers, and seek unity and peace. These commands don't cease when we become angry; rather, they require us to manage our anger constructively.

4

The Foundations of Anger

We want to avoid the destructive effects of anger. We don't want to be hurt by our own anger, to hurt others by our anger, or to be hurt by others who are angry. To avoid these problems we must understand where anger comes from, by forming some assumptions about the human condition.

The unifying feature of human beings is a drive toward wholeness in being and fullness in living. The drive toward wholeness means that, born as a "diamond in the rough," we desire to develop the beauty of our spirit that lies within and to protect it from harm. We express that desire as we seek to satisfy our physical needs for survival and protection, in the universal drive to fill the "God-shaped spiritual hole" in our beings, and in wanting to develop our natural abilities. This drive toward wholeness is a desire to attain a static condition of perfect completeness. We also strive toward a dynamic, active use of our being, by desiring a variety of experiences in life, and by producing things that are interesting, creative, meaningful, and fun.

However, an opposing force—sin—interferes. Sin, the result of rebellion against God, is everything that our drive toward wholeness is not. Sin seeks to disrupt our progress toward wholeness; its goal is the disintegration of our full lives. As sinful natural persons, we are pitifully weak against sin because Satan, director of the forces of sin, uses a million cunning ploys to divert us from our path toward completeness into stagnation, chaos, and destruction.

The environment in which we live has been fouled by sin. While it retains much of the exquisite beauty of God's creativity and shows the intricacies of His perfect design, it has been broken by sin to such an extent that it blocks the movement toward wholeness of Christian and nonbeliever alike. The environment creates circumstances to which the natural and inevitable responses are pain, fear, loneliness, despair, and anger.

Opposing Forces

So here are two forces: our innate drive toward completeness and perfection, and its opposite, named "sin," that seeks our fragmentation and destruction. Our lives are individual competitions between the drive toward wholeness and fullness and the organized and overwhelming forces of sin. The environment, the arena in which the contest is played, is rigged against us. We would have no hope of succeeding but for one thing—the possibility of partnership with God in this struggle. Without this we are doomed in the face of the powerful and persistent forces of sin.

God has given us freedom to choose the channels and means through which we will move in life. We can elect to use only those patterns and methods found in the natural world, or we can capitalize on God's resources. His resources include the wisdom of His word, the healing and inspiration that comes from our relationship with His Son, the comfort and direction of the Holy Spirit, the support of a loving community, and the empowerment of God Himself working through our lives. These resources make it possible for us to defeat the forces of sin and emerge victorious.

There are two implications for this that aid our study of anger. First, while both Christians and nonbelievers are subject to the tragedies of the environment, the Christian can use God's resources in coping and these resources make it possible to recover more quickly from the blows inflicted by the world.

The second implication is that the Christian does not need to complicate his own circumstances any longer by inviting sin into his life. By operating in harmony with God's order of living, the Christian matures and does less and less to bring disaster upon his own head. It is not the environmental conditions that wound us most severely, but our deficient responses to them.

What are the conditions that foster the response of anger? When we begin with the expression of anger and work backward to determine the conditions that preceded it, we find two main kinds of factors: (1) external forces that hammer our lives, and (2) internal conditions that are touched by those external forces.

External forces are conditions in our physical and social environment. The conditions that are particularly related to anger usually fall into one of these four categories: loss, threat, frustration, or rejection. These conditions generally cause feelings other than anger, for anger is not usually a primary feeling, but rather one that follows another feeling. Whether or not these conditions lead to a response of anger depends on the internal conditions.

When our dominant internal conditions include guilt, a sense of helplessness (from low self-esteem or lack of support), unrealistic expectations (from excessive self-esteem or a history of abuse of power), or aimlessness, the emotional response is likely to include anger, and it is probable that the angry individual will choose a destructive expression of it. When the internal conditions include an appropriate level of self-esteem, a mature understanding of life, and good relational skills, there is still likely to be anger—but either it will be identified as righteous indignation and be responded to accordingly, or the angry individual will choose to deal with the feeling of anger in other ways equally appropriate. Let us further define the external and internal conditions and then look at a case study.

External and Internal Conditions

The external condition of the loss of something or someone valuable often leads to anger. Some examples are the death of a loved one, loss of a home by a natural disaster, unemployment, physical incapacity, or children leaving home. The usual primary feelings are pain, sorrow, and grief, but these can easily turn to anger over the perceived injustice, the inconvenience, or the joy and excitement that are gone. Anger seeks a target so that, when the loss is caused by a general tragedy such as a natural disaster, the target of the anger is often God or persons who escape the tragedy.

Threats arise from a number of sources: competition in society, overcrowding, crime in the streets, rampant immorality, economic forces such as inflation, political forces such as nuclear proliferation, not being able to use job skills, or uncertainty about one's employability. The fact that we have no control over these social forces threatens us, leading to feelings of fear, anxiety, or insecurity. It is easy for us to become angry with whomever we perceive to be responsible for producing these feelings within us.

Frustration results when we are blocked from acquiring what we pursue. It is the feeling that arises most when our needs are not met. When we are frustrated we feel helpless, weak, and inadequate, and those feelings easily turn to anger. Ralph was frustrated in his attempt to drive home quickly after work; he felt powerless as he was trapped in the traffic jam.

Rejection may be the most agonizing emotional experience of all. Even in small doses it hurts. When we believe people are saying that we are not important or that they don't recognize our existence, we feel mortal, vulnerable, and worthless. These feelings easily turn to anger as we seek to retaliate against those whom we perceive as having caused it.

We expect more from our intimate relationships, so feelings of frustration and rejection will come more often from those we are closest to—and our emotional responses will be more intense. When our intimate friends disappoint or fail us, or when they seem to rebuff us or lose interest in us, conditions for anger build. In our story in chapter 2, Sally felt rejected when Ralph did not respond to her first call for dinner.

Each of us is continually confronted with external conditions such as these. Yet they do not always result in feelings of anger. What makes the difference? The difference lies in the conditions within us. There are several internal conditions that make it more likely that we will initially respond in anger and then not be able to manage the feelings of anger appropriately.

One internal condition is guilt. Guilt has its roots in original sin, but is nurtured by our own unconfessed and unrepented sins. Being guilty, we tend to retaliate and be intolerant and unforgiving. To be unforgiving adds another sin, and this increases our feelings of guilt.

The second condition is a sense of helplessness. This may be the result of deficient self-esteem or a lack of support, emotional or physical, from others. The roots of low self-esteem lie primarily in what is learned in childhood, especially within the family. It is nurtured by the sins of fear and self-rejection, and by the attention received from others for a "pity me" style of behavior.

When tragedy strikes, how good it is to be with those who care about us! How much more helpless we feel as we face harsh external conditions if we do not have supportive friends! Lack of support may occur because we have not taken the initiative to develop friendship in which we help one another, because we do not let others know what help we need, or because our helping friends are not available to assist when we need them or in the ways we need them.

A third internal condition is unrealistic expectations. This may be result from excessive self-esteem or a history of the abuse of power. Excessive self-esteem has its roots in childhood learning. It is nurtured when others reward angry behavior such as tantrums, and it is also fed by the sins of greed, conceit, selfishness, and pride.

Some persons seek a very high level of control over the environment and over other persons. They want to be in charge, to dominate, to "have the final say." As with other expressions of pride, the abuse of power may seem to be rewarding in the short run. There is a selfish satisfaction that comes from being number one or from being treated as royalty, but it is a false reward. The demanding behavior of the power-hungry person is most likely to bring out rebellion and resistance in other persons, increasing rejection, threat, frustration, and loss. Moreover, the basic attitude of insisting on supremacy is wrong. It is an expression of man's inherent sinful nature, a lineal descendant of Lucifer's challenge to the authority that God possesses and that He will never relinquish.

The final important internal condition is aimlessness. It has its roots in the failure to know that there can be no satisfying purpose without Christ. Aimlessness is nurtured by the distractions of sin in our broken world. What this means is that persons who have no true sense of mission in life, no real understanding of the meaning of their existence, and no clear sense of purpose are tremendously vulnerable to the vagaries of external conditions. Lacking a solid foundation for meaning in life, these persons are blown about by the changing winds of false ideas and faddish diversions.

Intermingled Conditions

Several internal and external conditions may be intermingled, as illustrated in the circumstances of a young woman who came to me for counseling. With tears streaming down her face and with anger in her voice, she talked about her husband. "The man's crazy, I tell you. He spends six to eight hours a day reading the Bible and yet the kids and I are scared half to death of him from the way he treats us. Does that make sense to you?"

It didn't. Her description of him reminded me of a few other people I've known, and the combination of time-consuming religious activity and ugly behavior never made sense. I usually felt angry around these people, but I preferred to stay neutral for the time being so I said, "Please tell me more about it."

"Well," she continued, "take last Sunday. We go to separate churches now. He won't go to the church we've always gone to, the one where we were married, anymore. He goes to this other church which he says is 'so much more spiritual.' Anyway, Sunday evening he asked the kids—he didn't ask me—if they wanted to go to church with him. When our son said he didn't want to, my husband, Bob said, 'I'll remember this the next time you want help with Boy Scouts.' Then when our daughter said she didn't want to go, he told her, 'The next time you want Jesus to do something, He won't.' Now, tell me something," she said, shaking her finger at me. "What kind of being religious do you call that?"

She certainly was angry, understandably. She was facing the external conditions of rejection, the threat of physical harm, the specter of possible psychological harm to the children, the frustration of not being able to help the family develop as a Christian unit, and the loss of companionship that she used to have with her husband. She was angry enough to want to divorce him.

His behavior suggested that he might feel angry as well, and this became apparent as he discussed his feelings. Some thirteen years earlier, in the first year of their marriage, he had had an extramarital affair. This created feelings of guilt and worthlessness, and he reverted to a primitive method for bolstering his sense of worth: fighting. By the time I met his wife, there had been nine years of physical abuse that had ended only when during one of his outbursts, he had thrown the family dog to the floor. His own rage had frightened him into the excessive religiosity his wife described, but his religious fervor had not borne the fruit of loving care for his family members.

His wife did not know how to do anything constructive about his fighting, and she could not physically fight back, so she retaliated with indirect, sneaky, aggressive behavior. This was subtle, but it effectively accomplished her purpose of keeping him in confusion and pain. For example, on one occasion when he had offered to take the family out for Sunday dinner after church, she took the children to a different restaurant ten minutes before he arrived home. Later she explained to him with phony innocence, "I thought you were going to meet us at the restaurant."

Another time, while they were out driving, she saw that he was forgetting to turn at the proper corner but waited until they were just through the intersection to say with feigned sweetness, "I thought you were going to turn there."

So, in his field of external conditions he had to contend with rejection from her, frustration in his efforts to do nice things for the family, loss of companionship, and the threat of her leaving. All of this combined with his real and exaggerated guilt feelings to contribute to his low self-esteem of long standing.

Her internal conditions included her feelings of guilt for her aggressiveness toward him, a history of low self-esteem, and a stubborn pride that refused to reconcile by meeting him halfway.

Willing to Forgive

How could this be resolved? Since he was willing to listen only to his own pastor and to God, we sought to incorporate the help of them both. The couple, his pastor, and I met together in God's presence in the pastor's office, and I confronted the couple with God's commands to forgive and His promises of forgiveness. I also described what would be required of them to restore their marriage and family relationships. They accepted God's offer of forgiveness and placed themselves under the authority of His commands. At that point their anger, a symptom of the deeper problems, began to diminish, and the internal conditions began a steady course of improvement.

This situation illustrates how intermingled the internal and external conditions in the lives of two persons can become. It also exemplifies how crucial it is to deal not only with symptoms but with changing basic internal conditions. It is not necessary, however, to understand the full history of a problem in order to resolve it. We do not need to know, for example, why he had the extramarital affair. Was she cunningly being aggressive toward him prior to that? Perhaps. It is unnecessary to try to unravel that old information.

It is essential, however, that each involved party honestly take the restorative actions that are needed: fulfilling responsibilities to God, to each other, and to self.

5

The Cycle of Anger

We have examined four internal conditions that make us vulnerable to becoming angry, and we have reviewed four categories of external conditions that press us from the outside. These conditions provide the opportunity for the emotional-physical-cognitive-behavioral phenomenon called anger to take place. With the ingredients in place, we will look at the recipe in more detail.

By studying the interplay between feelings and behavior we can increase our knowledge of anger. Let's examine this interplay in the story of Ralph and Sally related in chapter 2. We know that Ralph had a difficult day at work and that his drive home was very hectic (both affected by the behavior of others). He allowed himself to become increasingly tense and frustrated (his feelings in response to the events). When Ralph finally arrived home and had settled down in his easy chair (sensible behavior), he began enjoying, perhaps for the first time that day, a few moments of tranquillity (better feelings).

Ralph's tranquillity was interrupted by the call to dinner (behavior of others). The call to dinner was appropriate, but in the context of Ralph's day it seemed to him that once again he was being controlled by forces outside himself. He felt helpless (his primary feeling) and allowed that feeling to change to anger (secondary feeling), which in turn caused his outburst of yelling and kicking the paper (his choice of behavior).

Many behaviors intruded into Ralph's life. Some of those behaviors were his own, and some were the behaviors of others. These behaviors influenced Ralph's immediate feelings, and his feelings in turn influenced his subsequent behavior, which again influenced his feelings, and a sequence began that culminated in his angry explosion. What caused his explosion?

Under Pressure

Let's look at it by means of analogy. Suppose you have a balloon that is not inflated. Picture yourself holding the neck of the balloon between your fingers, the main part of the balloon dangling. Poke the balloon with a pin. What happens? Nothing. The balloon simply moves aside as the pin pushes it—no puncture, no bang.

Suppose now that you put just enough air in the balloon to enlarge it without stretching it. Poke it again with the pin: it still doesn't pop. It is amazing how much you can poke at the balloon without popping it. Now blow it up tightly. You know what will happen now if you touch it even slightly with a pin. Bang! What caused the explosion? The pin? No, the pressure inside creates the explosion and the sound. The balloon pops sooner if there is a pin, but it would also pop if the pressure were increased by blowing it up more.

When Ralph "popped," it was because of internal pressure, not the external pin of the call to supper. As Ralph faced conditions of threat and frustration during the day, he allowed pressure to increase within himself. Finally something happened that brought the pressure to a point he was not willing to tolerate, and he chose to explode.

The pattern is always similar. Pressure begins with a sense of rejection, loss, frustration, threat, or perhaps something else. It continues to build until something occurs that increases the pressure to a limit we will not tolerate, and then the stored-up emotional energy explodes within us in what we call "anger."

At this point there is a feeling, an explosion within us, but we have not exploded externally. We can easily explode outwardly if we chose to, but we do not have to. *We do have a choice!* We can explode with a tantrum, by attacking someone, or by throwing something. We can swallow our anger, letting it destroy us from within, or we can handle it constructively. We do have a choice about how the feeling of anger is expressed in behavior. We are morally responsible not to hurt ourselves or others, and we can accept that responsibility. Our loving God would not prohibit certain behaviors if it were impossible for us to control them.

When we become angry, our body is signaled by its autonomic nervous system to begin preparing for intense physical activity such as fighting or fleeing. We become equipped to "fly faster than a speeding bullet" or "leap over tall buildings at a single bound." Our body makes many changes such as speeding up the heart rate, breathing faster, and releasing sugar into the bloodstream. These enable the body to meet extreme physical demands. We do not have willful control over this physiological activation.

In most situations this physical supercharge is unnecessary. In fact, it may interfere with acting constructively toward the resolution of our anger. But it happens, and therefore we need to fit it properly into our response pattern.

We Decide

It is this tremendous burst of physical energy that makes it so dangerous to give physical expression to our anger. It is also dangerous for us to stuff the anger inside, thereby directing the physical energy against our own system. It is advantageous to avoid reaching the point where this involuntary physical response is triggered.

We have described three expressions of anger: destructive rage and resentment and constructive indignation. If the external conditions do not justify indignation, we must immediately begin a process of resolving the anger or it will take inappropriate expression as rage or resentment.

Our first decision is whether or not our response is one of indignation. This is how we can tell: Indignation is based in love. This is a fairly abstract rule to apply in the heat of an angry moment. A more complete and concrete description of indignation includes the following characteristics:

It can identify a real injustice;
It prays, not plots;

It points at a condition, not a person;
It helps the mistreated;
It teaches, rather than destroys, the offender;
It is unselfish;
It is often reluctant;
It refuses vengeance.

In reality, we make a decision about our next behavior instantaneously. We don't have time to pick up this book, deliberate over the list above, and write out a judicial opinion. So let's evaluate our behavior with this question: "Is my behavior a loving one?" Or, to put it another way, we should ask ourselves Charles Sheldon's famous question from *In His Steps*, "What would Jesus do?"

When our anger doesn't meet the criteria allowing us to respond with indignation, we must seek another appropriate means of handling it. Rage and resentment are off limits to us as Christians, and therefore we must learn to deal with our angry feelings before they take any of these forms. That fourth option is resolution.

Means of Control

Resolution requires that we control the expression of our impulses rather than being controlled by them. There are three important parts to this process:

1. First-aid techniques are helpful first steps in learning to resolve angry feelings. These are simple methods to get quick physical and emotional relief and to help us keep our behavior under control so we don't make things worse. They pave the way for doing something constructive about the causes of anger. Many people will practice first aid, feel better as a result, and

then decide that everything is all right and therefore they don't need to express anger. However, first aid is not enough by itself, because it does not produce lasting results.

2. We need to bring about a lasting cure. It is not enough to get relief from the misery of the moment; we also need to clean up the messes that are causing our misery. This involves resolving the causes and responding actively to adversity by working toward better conditions.

3. It is also important for us to learn to prevent anger whenever possible. We can't completely avoid anger, but much of our anger is unnecessary. It is our responsibility as Christians to reduce our vulnerability to commit sin and be controlled by it. Flirting with circumstances that bring forth responses of anger that we may not be able to deal with constructively is irresponsible for the Christian. Think again of the experiment with the balloon: In order to prevent future explosions, we must both deal with the sources of pressure and avoid unnecessary exposure to pins.

When we mature as Christians, our rate of success increases as we learn to respond to harsh circumstances around us by means other than anger. Things that we can do in prevention contribute to the improvement of our "batting average."

The time to exercise control is early, before the intensity of our anger gets too high. Anger, the most rapidly energizing emotion, becomes intense quickly. Resolution requires determined, willful response. We must take charge of emotions. Only when we are mature persons can we do this. We must recognize that rage and resentment will only complicate our lives further.

Chart I
THE CYCLE OF ANGER

CONDITIONS AND EVENTS	These are unpleasant experiences that are imposed on us (or on persons who are important to us) by a world marred by sin. The conditions of threat, rejection, loss, and frustration are especially likely to lead to anger responses.
INTERNAL CONDITIONS	The probability that one's response will include the feelings of anger increases when these internal conditions are present: guilt, sense of helplessness, unrealistic expectations, and aimlessness.

IMMEDIATE
RESPONSES

> Feeling of anger (we have a choice about this)
>
> Physical activation (no choice; controlled by autonomic system)
>
> Decisions: 1. Is it rage/resentment or righteous indignation?
> 2. Shall I respond destructively or constructively?

OPTIONS

	DESTRUCTIVE		CONSTRUCTIVE	
	Rage	Resentment	Resolution	Indignation
SUBSEQUENT WILLFUL RESPONSES	Tantrum, revenge attack	Bitterness, passive-aggressive behavior	"First aid" or "Cure"	Constructive actions to change unjust circumstances
WITH THE EFFECT OF:	Destroying others first, self later	Destroying self first, others later	Improving self and relations with others	Improving society; appropriately protecting self and others
EMOTIONAL-BEHAVIORAL LIFESTYLE	Domineering, hostile	Protective, suspicious	Prevention	Exposure
WHICH LEADS TO INTERNAL CONDITIONS:	Worse feelings, deteriorating self-esteem, confusion, weakened resistance to future harsh external conditions, guilt over wrong behavior		Better feelings, proper self-esteem, clearer purpose in life, mature emotional responses to future harsh external conditions, greater confidence and sense of freedom	

6

Destructive Styles of Dealing With Anger

Ralph and Sally illustrated the two basic destructive styles of expressing anger in behavior. One style is rage —to blow up and give in to feelings of anger quickly and vigorously. Ralph illustrated this dramatically when he yelled at Sally and kicked the newspaper.

Resentment is quite different. It holds angry feelings inside and denies them the verbal or physical expression they seek. Sally did this when she chose to remain silent, not even responding to Ralph's overture to talk ("I'm sorry. Are you asleep?") that might have led to healing of the incident. She held her anger inside as long as she could, not expressing it until the following day when she retaliated against Ralph's anger by serving him cold mashed potatoes.

Both styles are destructive because they attack. Ralph attacked Sally verbally and attacked the newspaper physically. Sally attacked herself first and then attacked Ralph indirectly. Both styles are impractical because they break down human relationships that need to be strong and positive. In both styles we are controlled by our feelings, rather than controlling them so that we are free to act on the basis of purposeful belief. Both rage and resentment are subchristian expressions of anger because they are motivated by selfishness rather than by servanthood.

The destructiveness of expressing anger in rage is extremely common. At the most vicious level it is manifest in murder, rape, child abuse, and other extreme antisocial behavior. When we express anger physically, we usually abuse objects rather than people—Ralph kicked the newspaper, for example. We tend to throw things or to pound a fist against something. We also express rage verbally with temper tantrums, screaming, criticizing, condemning, sarcasm, and various forms of name calling.

A Bad Chain Reaction

Even the milder forms of these behaviors are likely to set off a bad chain reaction. They are likely to lead to loss of friendship and to rejection by others. We may embarrass ourselves because of our behavior in front of others, and that, in turn, may lead to self-criticism and shame. In addition, open verbal conflict usually creates resentment and invites others to retaliate. It keeps our problems going rather than seeking their solution. Conflict leads to behavior that is clearly wrong and which makes us truly guilty. Furthermore, anytime there is verbal hostility there is the possibility of physical violence. Scripture clearly condemns all these behaviors. Read the verses below and summarize your conclusions.

Romans 12:19
Matthew 5:39
Proverbs 14:17; 15:18; 29:20, 22

The destructiveness of rage in our relationships with others is seen in the experience of Burt, a forty-year-old man. Burt's earliest memory is of being sick as a child, with a fever of 104 degrees. He remembers his mother sponging him with cold water to reduce his temperature during the night and sobbing, "I wish I never had this kid, I wish I never had this kid." Burt remembers vividly his mother saying such things as "I wish you were never born" . . . "I wish you had never seen the light of day" . . . "You'll never amount to a hill of beans" . . . "You can never do anything right."

Burt, an only child, remembers virtually no emotional support from either parent. He says, "I was so alone. Nobody cared, and if they did, I still thought they didn't. I never received recognition for doing anything right, but I got a lot of attention for doing wrong."

Somewhere along the way Burt discovered that he could manipulate his father by having tantrums. Burt says, "Although my father had a lot of rules, I found I could wear him out with anger. I'd shout a little and threaten to leave home or quit school, and he'd give in. It worked."

This manipulative behavior didn't work for Burt in adult life. He showed the self-defeating nature of his angry responses in this incident he related to me: "I'm miserable all the time, so I guess I want others to be miserable too. One night my friend Dewey came over and wanted me to go out for pizza with him. He

Destructive Styles of Dealing With Anger

suggested a place, but I said, 'That place isn't any good,' and started running the place down just to get his goat. So Dewey said, 'Okay, then don't go,' and he left. There I was, angry with him although I knew I shouldn't be, and angry with myself for making a mess out of things again. It seems as if I've done that a million times and it hasn't ever hurt anybody more than it has hurt me."

On another occasion, Burt got home from work and his wife wasn't there with supper on the table as was customary. Burt began to feel rejected and angry. His wife came home a few minutes later.

"Where have you been?" Burt roared.

She had been next door where the neighbor's dog had just borne a litter of pups, but responding to Burt's anger she said, "I don't have to tell you! I'm a married woman, big enough to come and go as I please."

"You're the wife here, and your job is to have supper on the table!" Burt shot back. "I don't have to stay here if this continues."

"You don't have the guts to leave!" she taunted. "There isn't any place or anybody that would have you anyway."

Burt's anger controlled him, and within five minutes he was walking toward his car with a suitcase in hand. *This will teach her,* he thought.

Contrary to his expectations, it taught her how pleasant life could be without him. She wouldn't let him come back. Burt also learned from this experience, and his relationships with others have improved, but . . . his wife still doesn't want him back. That's something Burt says he'll regret as long as he lives. Rage doesn't work. Other people won't put up with it.

Resentment, the other common style of dealing destructively with angry feelings, holds them inside. We destroy ourselves rather than others, and from a Christian point of view this is just as wrong.

Many Christians choose to hold angry feelings inside. If this is so destructive, why do they do it? Because people who express their anger outwardly are usually condemned for it, while people who quietly swallow dissatisfaction and stifle their anger are subtly reinforced. In our culture, women have been under considerable social pressure not to show anger, while men have been allowed more freedom to express their anger. Society forbids us to hurt others with our anger, and as Christians we are aware of the sinfulness of attacking others. Society allows us to hurt ourselves with our anger without restraint, however. On the whole, the church has not instructed us concerning the sinful response to anger. Most people don't realize that it's harmful to keep anger unexpressed and thus allow us to take it out on ourselves.

Sometimes we *must* swallow our feelings of anger, but we cannot do this permanently without damage to ourselves and to our relationships with others. There is a lot of energy in anger, and that energy does destructive things to us physically and emotionally if it is not neutralized or given opportunity for constructive expression.

Suppressing anger has unpleasant side effects for us emotionally. We may worry, thinking that we won't be able to continue to hold in our anger. We must learn that worrying is unnecessary. We do not have to live in fear of our feelings of anger, because we do not need to be controlled by them. We can learn ways of dealing with our feelings of anger that are better than either blowing up or suppressing them.

Guilt feelings may come as another side effect of suppressing anger. We may feel guilty about feeling angry because we think anger is wrong. These guilty feelings are usually not justified.

Emotionally, suppressing anger is like stuffing tennis balls into a trunk. At first they fit easily, but eventually the trunk gets full. As we squeeze more tennis balls in, it gets hard to close the lid. We pile them up and press hard on the lid to keep it shut. But every time we open the lid to stuff more in, a few spill out. It takes more and more energy to keep the lid down, because the balls push back as though to force their way out.

The person who is putting a lot of energy into keeping the lid on suppressed anger is greatly inhibited in the ability to live life joyfully. When we are handcuffed by suppressed anger, we cannot be our natural selves. This makes us less interested in other people and less attractive to others, and it reduces the amount of satisfaction we get from being with others.

Persons who suppress anger are more prone to depression than those who deal with it properly. Anger does not cause depression, but it is often an early warning sign and a complicating factor.

The risk of illness is increased because of the destructive physical side effects of anger. We may be able to tolerate the tension that anger provides right now, but it will take its toll sometime. It is beneficial to learn response patterns that will reduce the stress of anger. If we learn to handle anger now, it will be helpful to us for the rest of our lives.

Anger Toward Oneself

Resentment also hurts our relationships with others. Stuffing the anger inside as a destructive act toward self increases our bitterness toward ourselves. That bitterness usually gets generalized to others, which complicates the relationships that are needed for healthy living. We often put ourselves down for suppressing anger instead of taking care of it, and our feeling of failure may well be justified.

Anger that is held in always hurts us. Do you know persons who suffer because they have not learned how to deal constructively with their anger? Chuck is an example of how extremely unhealthy anger toward oneself can be.

Chuck sat hunched over on the edge of his chair, eyes on the floor. His broad shoulders slouched inward as his stocky fingers dug roughly through his heavy, unruly hair. The deep lines in his face made him look far older than his thirty-eight years.

"My trouble began when I was born, and it's all been downhill since then." Chuck laughed, but I knew that he believed every word. There was probably a relentless churning inside, as if a hundred demons with battering rams were pounding him.

"My life has been miserable. One disappointment after another . . . one rotten disappointment after another. I'm a 'born loser.' The original, the one they named the comic strip after." His grin tired to make light of the disgust he was feeling for himself, but he hurt deeply inside.

Destructive Styles of Dealing With Anger

Chuck's veins throbbed with tension against the skin of his forehead. I felt my own body tighten as the intensity of Chuck's despair pressed against me, but I wasn't prepared for what happened next. Chuck raised his white-knuckled fist and slammed it full force into his stomach. He gasped, "I'm no good! Just no stinkin' good!" Feelings of his agony seemed to knock the breath out of *me*. Chuck's despairing expression told me he believed what he said.

He leaned toward me, saying angrily, "There isn't one good reason why I should live!" He flopped back into his chair with a painful sigh. As he shook his head slowly from side to side, tears rolled down his cheeks.

Now I wanted, more than I can tell you, to help Chuck. I didn't know him very well. We were together that weekend for an educational workshop: he was a participant and I the leader. He had impressed me from the start, for it was evident that others who knew him well respected him and liked him. I also learned that Chuck was successful as a junior high school teacher and had a very positive impact on his students.

I described my impressions to him. "Chuck, you're a powerful man—physically and emotionally. You have powerful punches, whether those are physical punches or emotional punches, and you hit yourself both ways. The way you explained how lousy your life has been has to be more than you can bear. Now you're caught in the middle of it and wondering if it's worth continuing, I'd like to talk about that with you if you want to."

Chuck nodded and began talking at length. He told about being pushed around at home and about how hard he worked to earn a thank-you from his father without ever receiving one. He told me that years later his father sold a farm and divided the money with Chuck's two brothers, saying, "Chuck doesn't deserve anything. He's a lazy teacher who works only nine months a year, so he doesn't deserve anything."

"Chuck, did you ever talk about these things, or these feelings, with your Dad?" I asked.

"No."

"With anyone?"

"No."

Rejection, the seed of anger, had grown into resentment and was now ripening into bitter fruit in Chuck's life. It resulted in alcohol abuse, an ulcer, hypertension, conflict with his own children, and suicidal impulses. Chuck's childhood should have been different, but he couldn't control that; so his response to the rejection needed to be different, and learning how was something he could control.

Releasing the Tension

The biggest problem with suppressing anger is that it doesn't stay suppressed. Somehow we know that internalized anger destroys us, so our system tires to get some release from the tension. Often this results in an attack on the person we believe to be responsible for our injury. Because we believe it would be wrong to retaliate directly—and so reject that alternative—we cleverly devise ways to retaliate without being consciously aware of it. Sally loved Ralph and wouldn't consider attacking him directly, but she did let herself sneak in a mild jab with the cold mashed potatoes.

There are many devious ways to attack. One method is passive-aggression, which involves not doing something that should be done. This can really frustrate the person we attack because our alibi is "Don't blame me—I didn't do anything!"

A man in the shipping room of a small mail-order company, for example, cost the owner hundreds of customers before it was discovered that he was holding orders for two weeks before filling them. He was working hard and smiling on the outside, but he was extremely angry on the inside. "But boss! I've been working so hard!" was his response.

Another case concerns a teacher who saw water leaking from a drinking fountain on the second floor when she was leaving the school for the weekend. Her first thought was to stop by the office, until she remembered how angry she was with the principal. *That's her problem,* the teacher thought. The leaking water caused the ceiling of the room below to collapse. "Don't blame me—I didn't do anything!" said the teacher.

Other clues to passive-aggression include chronic tardiness, obstructionism (the committee member who is against everything), sloppiness of performance or personal grooming, low sexual responsiveness, obesity, and procrastination. This type of aggression can become the major focus of one's life.

Another story illustrates the sad results of this type of behavior. Four-year-old Esther was given the job of taking care of her younger brother. One warm and sunny day he wanted to go to the railroad tracks and play with stones. The two of them sat down between the rails, digging out pretty rocks from between the ties and throwing them out.

Esther got thirsty and went back to the house for a drink, telling her brother she would "be right back."

While she was gone, a freight train thundered by, killing her little brother. Esther found his lifeless body still between the tracks.

That happened forty-five years ago. Esther remembers her brother's death being mentioned only once at home, but for forty-five years she was painfully aware of being treated differently in the family than the way her two brothers and two sisters were.

Despite this treatment she coped rather well. She worked as a secretary for twelve years before she put herself through college, then she held a professional position with the same organization for fifteen years. Suddenly, shockingly, she was unemployed. She was confronted with the frustration of looking for a suitable job, uncertain whether she would be able to find one that would use and reward her abilities. She faced the prospect of a life of loneliness as a single person. These situational factors would be difficult for any of us, but she was especially vulnerable because of her years of self-doubt, self-criticism, guilt, feelings of unworthiness, and lack of emotional support from her family.

Esther became intensely aware of the clear but subtle belittling and rejecting attitudes her family had expressed to her over the years. Her family blamed Esther for her brother's death and had never forgiven her. She realized that she had been a scapegoat and an outlet for the frustrations of every other family member. Yet she had held up remarkably well in the face of thousands of messages over the years that told her she was inadequate and unworthy. Now everything had caught up with her. She was tired of persisting.

She responded in two ways: She became depressed, and she moved into her sister's home. She didn't ask, she didn't knock, she just moved in, lock-stock-and-barrel. Her sister and her brother-in-law looked up and there she was. "Woe is me; things are terrible!" she whined and pouted, demanding sympathy. She phoned the other sister and brothers to say, "I'm helpless. I can't do a thing. Help me! Help me!"

It's a tough way to get even, but that is what was happening. How hard it was for Esther to understand and accept that her depression was a form of attack against her family.

The Disguise of Humor

Humor is another way to disguise aggression. Some authors say all humor is aggressive. A lot of it is, but it does not have to be. Much of the humor on TV situation comedies is hostile. It is based on cheap and degrading sacrasm, ethnic slurs, sexist slander, or obscenity. An artificial laugh track conditions us into believing we're being entertained, when in fact we are being insulted. We ought to hear the canned laughter as derision of our stupidity for continuing to listen.

We pull a lot of self-esteem out of being thought humorous or clever, so we try to get laughs anyway we can. Whether it means an insult, being crude, or getting lifted up by putting others down, anything is acceptable. We're hurting for respect so we fire any cheap shot that will get a quick ho-ho, and we hope the sound of the laughs will mask the crudeness of our jokes.

When I was in junior high school, one of my teachers said to the class, "Walters could do anything if he put his mind to it." The class was deathly quiet. On the outside I was embarrassed, but on the inside I was proud. Then the teacher added, "Morton could too, if he had a mind." The class laughed uproariously. On the outside Morton laughed hardest of all, but on the inside . . . ? It must have been funny: they all laughed. Baloney!

What's the real meaning when a person greets a friend with "Hi, turkey!" Does a word like "turkey" carry friendship? Healthy competitiveness? Compulsive competitiveness? Animosity? Is "turkey" just a sound with no meaning at all?

I have asked people about this. Most seem uncomfortable with the question and quickly say it's no big deal: "Friends know that no harm is intended." They claim that it is a way of showing affection without getting mushy. The expression reaps good feelings, they say, not bad. But many times, after thinking about it, they say they really don't like it. At best, they say, it leaves you wondering why the person used a put-down instead of a lift-up.

Labels That Degrade

Dingbat, Peon, Dummy, Frump, Oddball, Clown, Meathead: Do labels like these diminish the target person? Perhaps. More so, they diminish the person who uses them, because to the extent that they describe the other as less valuable, we are also degraded. It is in *giving* to others that we become strong, not in taking away.

A friend introduced me to his five-year-old son. Father said, "He's kind of a wet noodle, but we love him." The boy, blushing, stared intently at the floor. So did everyone but father, who laughed nervously. That was twenty years ago. Fortunately the put-down didn't seem to hurt the son. That little boy is now a confident self-starter; he's successful and happy in what he does. Maybe it doesn't matter, but why use a label when you could use a medal?

I like affirmation. Even the plain old run-of-the-mill kind. Just your basic, no-frills, economy affirmation suits me. It doesn't have to have a designer's tag. I'll pick a plain affirmation over a sterling silver insult any day of the week—especially on Sunday.

Inappropriate joking even happens at church. One Sunday Mary introduced her sister Rachel to a man. The man said, "If you're Mary's sister, we better pray for you right away." He laughed; but they didn't. I wasn't sure if he had insulted one or both of them. Then I met the man and he introduced me to Ben. I mentioned that I had met Ben before, at a convention. The man said to me, "Well, you must of got off lucky. It looks like it didn't hurt you none." He laughed but Ben didn't. I felt uncomfortable.

It is clear in Scripture what is acceptable and what is not. Paul says, "Do not let any unwholesome talk come out of your mouths, but only what is helpful for building others up according to their needs, that it may benefit those who listen" (Eph. 4:29). "Benefit those who listen? I want everything to benefit me!" is a natural response. It's a simple rule to understand, but hard to apply because we do not see many examples of humor that build up. Practice.

Most Christians do not deliberately choose destructive expressions of anger; it happens by default. We want to choose the positive response of resolution of our anger but we're not confident that it will turn out successfully. Holding our anger in seems safer, so we do that and hurt ourselves. Sensing what we have done, we now feel worthless, hurting ourselves even more and giving us one more thing to be angry about. The alternative is to learn acceptable response styles and, with God's help, to incorporate those proper responses as part of a Christlike life style.

Anger can be dangerous. It can devour us. It can eat us alive from the outside by destroying relationships and by complicating our lives, or it can destroy us from the inside. It is dangerous, but we can learn to deal with it confidently.

7

"First Aid" Methods of Coping With Anger

Sometimes anger strikes like a headache in a television commercial and we need "fast relief." At this moment we have a chance to bring the anger cycle to a screeching halt, or at least to keep ourselves under control so that we don't cause things to get worse.

The "first aid" techniques will help us feel a little better. They will help us "buy some time" to settle down and plan what to do next. They are valuable to counter the effects of the fight/flight syndrome which makes it difficult to deal logically with the situation. But the first aid methods don't take care of everything that needs to be done. We need to go beyond them to understand why we got angry in the first place and to do the things we can do to deal with those causes of anger. This is discussed in more detail in the next chapter.

What we can do depends on the circumstances we are in, so we need to know a variety of techniques to choose from. None of these, of course, is more than a temporary measure.

Let's look at these techniques in three categories: those that capitalize on God's desire to help us, those that use our human willful control, and those that allow us to release some of the physical and emotional tension. Then we'll mention a few actions and attitudes that should be avoided.

Asking for God's Help

The first group of these methods focuses primarily on asking God for His help with our attitudes. Attitudes, which can be right or wrong, have great influence on behavior.

We can learn to recognize that God is in control. God's sovereignty over the universe has not been overruled by the events that have caused our anger. God will never be overruled—He is in control! He has always known about and is allowing everything that is happening to you. Note what these verses say about the source of our strength and hope: Psalms 29:11; 46:10; Matthew 11:28-29.

We can learn to pray with thanksgiving and praise. This goes beyond knowing that God is in control to exalting Him for it. The familiar opening words of the Lord's Prayer serve well: "Our Father in heaven, hallowed be your name" (Matt. 6:9).

We can learn to pray for peace in our hearts. We must ask for the Christlike quality that is the opposite of the sinful characteristic troubling us. For example, if we are angry we must ask for peace. It works with any sinful problems, because for each there is a divinely ordered opposite that is to be our ideal. So, if the problem is resentment, we must ask for love; if jealousy, brotherhood; if lust, purity; if doubt, faith.

We can learn to pray for the person. To pray on behalf of a person with whom you are angry, in a supportive way and without condemnation, marks a commitment to forgive. Honestly done, it is an unselfish act of love—and since love is the most powerful force, it will ultimately triumph.

We can read and think about Scripture. Mental and emotional renewal often takes place through displacement. As we are filled with wholesome new thoughts and feelings, the unhealthy old ones are crowded out. Better than bringing in neutral thoughts, as described later, is to introduce God's own Word.

Human Willful Control

God readily helps when we seek His help. He has also designed us for a great deal of self-sufficiency and expects us to use the processes and resources that are part of His design. This group of suggestions includes simple, specific ways to use what God has given us.

We can measure the issue. We should obtain a reasonably accurate perspective on the issue, asking ourselves, "Is it worth it to get angry about this?" Let's decide not to waste energy being angry over trivia.

We can control ourselves. We must cool down by using our self-control. It is possible. Did you ever have an argument interrupted by a phone call? Your behavior changed immediately. On the telephone you were polite and sensible, but then when you hung up, you went back into a rage. When you had to, you controlled your behavior. We usually can if we decide to.

What would we do if we were throwing a silly tantrum

and the President of the United States walked up to us, or if network television cameras were suddenly aimed on us? We might not relax, but we'd probably shape up. Pretend this is happening.

Controlling ourselves begins by deciding that we want to control it; then moderating our behavior will help. Speak softly: talking quietly has a calming effect on us, just as it will on the other person.

We must remind ourselves that an angry feeling is okay. We must not put ourselves down for feeling angry unless we are choosing to be angry or choosing to stay that way. Agreeing to deal completely with the feeling and taking care of the things that are causing it as well as we can and as soon as we can are crucial. Then we're off the hook. When we are angry already, we don't need unproductive self-criticism.

Getting our mind on something else—anything else —helps by turning our attention from the problem to something neutral or noncontroversial. This, like the use of all other "first aid" methods is a momentary diversion while the effects of the "fight/flight syndrome" subside. There are many ways to do it.

Maintaining Positive Thoughts

The most common anger-control suggestion is counting. The reason this is so common is because it works. Thomas Jefferson said, "When angry count ten before you speak; if very angry, a hundred." This is good advice, although he didn't mention that some of us may need to count to 142,000. Or, recite the alphabet backward, or count backward from 200 by sevens.

Maintaining positive thoughts makes anger easier to handle. Picturing ourselves working through the problem that arouses our anger and visualizing success involves positive thinking. Direct your attention to your surroundings, noticing the textures of objects, counting the number of colors we see around us, or paying attention to what we usually ignore. Think of beautiful, happy scenes: recall a gorgeous sunset, a scenic spot you have enjoyed, or your most memorable Christmas tree. Most of all, we should remember to count our blessings. The purpose of these thoughts is to move our attention temporarily from the irritant to something neutral or pleasant.

Separating ourselves from the conflict sometimes helps. Many times we can't do that, but we should if we can. If no one else is involved at the moment we are angry, it is helpful to get a change of scene. If someone is, we can probably excuse ourselves "to go get a drink of water." If we're so emotionally excited with the situation that we can't deal with it sensibly, it is better to ask for postponement of a conversation than to proceed destructively. Sooner or later we need to come back and come to grips with the issue, for there is no point in trying to hide from it forever; but getting away from the scene for a little while can be very helpful.

If we want to leave, we should ask if we can talk about the problem later. Nevertheless, when we postpone, we must be sure to suggest a specific time so our leaving doesn't look like a put-off. We might say, "This is important to me, but it's hard for me to talk about it right now. Can we talk about it at ——?" (and you suggest a specific time). This may annoy the other person a little, but it's probably far better than charging ahead and making a bigger mess of things.

If you decide to leave, don't drive! While no one knows

for sure what proportion of automobile accidents are caused by angry drivers, recent reports suggest that it may be as many as one out of three. There isn't any debate about the fact that when we are angry, we are not physically in a condition to drive a car or operate other dangerous equipment.

Releasing the Tension

The following methods help us relieve some of the pressure gradually in acceptable ways. Again, we must note that these activities are not a totally satisfactory response to anger, but they can help temporarily.

Doing something we enjoy, such as listening to our favorite music, is relaxing. Sing: the physical and mental involvement of making a joyful noise is incompatible with anger.

We can channel our energy into something constructive. When we're angry, our bodies are prepared for intense activity. We can let that energy out in useful ways by doing something physical. Anything constructive that we can do to let off some of our physical charge is helpful. We may even want to tackle a difficult job that we've been postponing: scrubbing a floor, cleaning the garage, pulling weeds, or doings something that we've been afraid to do. In the angry state, we are better equipped for simple physical tasks than for resolving things with the person we're angry with; so we should use this "worked-up" physical and emotional state to do something that is needed. While we are angry about the neighbor's dog, writing a letter to our congressman about one of the things we're indignant about or writing a letter to the newspaper editor can help us let off some steam.

"First Aid" Methods of Coping With Anger

Best of all, we can do something constructive for someone else, letting our emotions work for us and keeping us out of harm's way while the physical/emotional energy subsides.

Talk with a friend. We all need a person in life who will listen to us when we are at our ugliest and who will care about us and respect us anyway. (And we do the same for them.) By using the listening ear of that friend, spouse, teacher, or pastor in a sensible and constructive way, we can unload our sense of frustration. The frustration needs to get cleared away so that action to restore and improve the broken situation can begin. Just don't ask your friend to clean up the mess for you!

Talk with yourself. Do it alone and do it out loud. But I did not say, "Talk *to* yourself." No, we need dialogue, so we get to answer ourselves as well! You will be delighted how trivial many big problems sound when talked about out loud. Try it in front of a mirror.

A similar method is to write it down. This is another fine way to improve your perspective of the problem. Put down on paper what you feel and why. Try a letter to the person with whom you are angry—but don't mail it. Read it the next morning, and you will probably laugh and be ashamed; but at the time you can deal prayerfully with the basic problem.

Laughter is good medicine. Our sense of humor gets lost when we're angry. Laughing and anger are basically incompatible. What can we find to do that will make us laugh and thus displace anger? We can laugh at ourselves when we are angry—it's one of the healthiest things we can do.

Crying is also a legitimate form of release. Tears can

wash away psychological irritants just as they may wash away a speck of dust that irritates the eye. But don't let the process of resolving the problem end with the tears; move ahead with the problem solving until the tears of frustration or hurt are replaced by tears of celebration.

Letting Go of Trivia

It is important for us to learn to let go of the trivia. "A man's wisdom gives him patience; it is to his glory to overlook an offense" (Prov. 19:11). "Do not pay attention to every word people say . . ." (Eccl. 7:21).

We can ask ourselves, "What's the worst possible thing that can happen?" We are likely to see that even the worst thing that could happen is not bad enough to get upset over. We might take this a step further by deliberately exaggerating more and more to take the consequences to their absurd extreme.

Relax. Anger and relaxation are incompatible. If we experience one, we can't experience the other, so let's displace anger with relaxation. Do something nice for your body, such as soaking in a hot tub and letting the anger and tension go down the drain with the bath water. Lie down. How angry can we be flat on our back? Physical relaxation assists emotional relaxation. Breathing deeply and slowly is also relaxing: take a deep breath, hold it for a second, then exhale slowly. You will want to exhale quickly, but breathing slowly is more relaxing. Do this five times. Muscle relaxation is a skill that you can learn, just as you might train your body in other skills.

Such things as hitting a punching bag, wadding newspapers, ripping apart an old bath towel, or screaming and pillow pounding are useful for persons who are not able to release anger in any other way yet need to learn how under controlled, supervised circumstances such as psychotherapy. These methods are probably harmless or even helpful when not used to excess; but I prefer putting the energy of anger into something useful rather than practicing something I don't really need to know how to do.

I am firmly opposed to activities that simulate destroying the person with whom one is angry, such as throwing darts at an image of the person or destroying that person in mental fantasy. These activities are incompatible with Christianity, and the scientific data shows that such practices increase rather than decrease aggressiveness.

Cautions

While it is important to deal with anger quickly, there are two dangers to avoid during the "first aid" phase when responding to the feeling of anger:

1. Do not make important decisions while angry. Our ability to think clearly is reduced while we are angry.

2. Do not make judgments about people. Remember that we can change only ourselves. Concentrate on that instead of thinking about how we would like to change others.

The intensity of the physiological response and the length of time before it subsides vary greatly from person to person. Do not let it drag out longer than necessary. Move into the process of "cure" as soon as you can.

8

Cure: Resolving Circumstances That Encourage Anger

Anger is a symptom of problems within us or around us. It is not enough just to get relief from the misery of the moment; we need to clean up the mess that is causing the misery. We dare not let anger accumulate or let the conditions that produce it go unchallenged.

Quieting a lifetime of rage or resentment isn't as simple as whipping up a batch of instant grits, but even a small start is an improvement on living with anger-born hassles. We can take some steps that will help us move toward lasting change.

It is crucial for us to learn to ask God to assist us in this process. Scripture encourages us to seek God's help with our problems, and assures us that we will receive it. My personal experience in seeking God's help with the problems and confusion of life bears this out, and if you have ever asked God for help, you know about His dependable power, too. Praise God! Just a few of the verses that promise us His help are Isaiah 43:2–3; Jeremiah 29:12–13; John 14:26; 16:13; Romans 8:26–28; Philemon 4:6–7; Hebrews 13:5–6; James 1:5.

First of all, we must be aware of anger. We cannot resolve it until we acknowledge it. As long as we don't accept it, there is an additional internal conflict of pretending it is not there. If anger is present, recognizing it cannot hurt us, but denying it can.

Secondly, it is necessary to undo any damage we have done to the extent it is possible. Sometimes we become angry because someone has hurt us in retaliation for what we have done. We need to ascertain whether this is the case, and if we are at fault, we must begin to straighten it out as well as we can, as soon as we can.

Apology and Restitution

This means to apologize, take responsibility for what we have done, and express our intention not to repeat it. An apology is a sign of personal strength. Restitution may also be required. Restitution means doing whatever we can to restore conditions to what they were or to what they might have been had it not been for our transgression. We cannot do this completely, but we must do the best we can.

When we discover that we have been in the wrong, we should say so in a simple and straightforward way. For example, we might say, "I should not have said that about you. My statement was misunderstood, and you've been hurt by that. I'm sorry." Then we should go on to find out if there is need for restitution: "Is there anything I can do to help get the misunderstanding straightened out?"

There are times when we need to apologize only for part of what happened. For example, we may not need to retract our opinion even though we apologize for the way in which we expressed it: "I'm sorry about the way I flew off the handle when I found out that you borrowed my lawnmower without asking. I should have been more polite when I talked to you."

If an apology or restitution is necessary, it should be made right away. The Bible clearly states that we are to make amends for our wrong actions promptly (Matt. 5:23–26). Ask yourself right now, "Do I have anything I need to take care of with anyone?" Think especially about those persons closest to you.

Parents, do not hesitate to apologize to your children when it is in order. Our example is the most effective way to teach our children the power of humility. Our apology will give closure to our injury to them and will build a stronger relationship.

We must also evaluate our anger and decide what our response should be: resolution or indignation. We shouldn't channel our anger into indignation unless there is an injustice to ourselves or to others. We must resolve the feeling of anger if we cannot positively identify an injustice—e.g., we may think people are talking about us.

—Or if the injustice is insignificant—e.g., the newspaper was delivered an hour later than usual.

—Or if the injustice is only perceived as injustice when in reality it is something else, such as disappointment—e.g., it rained on your birthday;

—Or if we cannot do anything constructive about the injustice—e.g., our canary was struck by lightning;

—Or if the benefits of our constructive action would

be offset by reduction in usefulness in another area of life—e.g., we get so upset crusading against child abuse that we become harmfully protective of our own children.

Fanning the Flame

Once we decide whether our response should be resolution or indignation, we must not let our anger grow. Ask yourself whether you are looking for a fire extinguisher or fanning the flame. Look for attitudes or internal messages that keep it going. For example, we may be thinking such things as "Those clowns take advantage of me every time they get a chance!" or we may be saying to ourselves, "You dummy, why do you let people push you around like that—it's no wonder your life is a mess!" That kind of irrational thinking is no good. Don't do it!

At this point we should vocally renounce the inappropriate options. Do this before God and before other persons. Simply say something like, "I refuse to be controlled by my anger. I am going to understand where this unpleasant feeling comes from and do the proper things to deal with it."

Bring your anger into perspective by finding and analyzing its source. In this analytical process it can be very useful to have the help of a friend. We can do a lot on our own, but consulting a friend, a pastor, or a professional counselor may be desirable.

There are a couple of techniques that might help us understand our own personal response to anger. First of all, try word association. Write down all the words that come into your mind when you think of the word *anger.* This will give you some grist for your mental mill

77

as you seek to understand where your anger is coming from.

Second, keep an "anger diary card." Carry a small card with you for a few weeks, and every time you feel a little angry, write down what is happening. You might do this with abbreviations and initials, writing things down so that anyone else finding the card won't know what it's all about. This will give you freedom to keep track of things on the card. After two or three weeks you will probably have accumulated enough data to analyze it, looking for trends that may tip you off to what is causing the irritable and angry feelings. You may not get a list of causes, but at least you will have a list of situations. Pray to understand the underlying meanings of each of these.

Finally, we must seek to understand what purpose our anger is serving. How does it benefit us? Are we controlling others with it? If so, they will rebel against it as soon as they can. Are we getting attention with anger? There are better ways, for our anger will soon be ignored. Do we get a sneaky thrill out of nursing revenge? That's wrong, so naturally that won't feel good for long.

After we have analyzed our anger, we must begin planning constructive actions to deal with it. Conditions in our personal lives seldom change without purposeful action.

It is often up to us to take the initiative in gaining a happy life. "He must turn from evil and do good; he must seek peace and pursue it" (1 Peter 3:11). We must turn, we must seek, and we must take responsibility to act upon our circumstances, not sit idly back and wait for things to change.

Taking the initiative involves expressing to the appropriate person exactly how we feel. We should do this in person in an assertive style. This is a "report," to acknowledge to the other person that we feel angry, and in no way should we blame or condemn him or her. Rather, we are taking responsibility for how we feel and doing something about those feelings.

We must confront the person about the behavior that has made us angry. That's tough. But it is essential, and in the long run it is best. Consider the message of these verses: Proverbs 27:5; 28:23; Luke 17: 1–4. Scripture tells us a lot about how to confront others appropriately and successfully; but the full development of that topic is beyond the scope of this book.

If a number of people are involved in an angry situation, we should arrange a group meeting. With everyone present, we must pray for courage to want the truth, caring enough for each other to express it, having the discernment to recognize it, and having the wisdom to know how to use it. We must talk freely about individual goals and needs, and seek ways to fulfill the needs of others.

Forgiving Is Crucial

The final and most crucial step in neutralizing anger's destructive power is forgiving. Anger often comes because of neglect or mistreatment from others. The way to resolve this is by forgiving others for what they have done to us. There is tremendous, exciting power available to us in forgiving, as we will discover in the next chapter. As God's power flows through us to help us forgive others, there comes a healing of the wounds of the past. Forgiving is, without doubt, the most important part of the resolution of anger.

As part of this process we can ask the person with whom we are angry to help us understand and resolve the anger in the relationship. This calls for good communication, the desire for dialogue, willingness to see ourselves in new ways, and the capacity for constructive change in our behavior and attitudes.

Misunderstanding the other person's intentions or regard for us is likely to occur if we do not know the person very well. This increases our susceptibility to anger. Friendship often changes this, so it is important to cultivate friendship whenever possible. This is especially helpful in regard to those whom we do not know very well.

Having now identified the situations that cause anger, taken care of our part of it, and confronted other persons, if any, about their responsibility in the matter, we need to seek to structure matters so that they will be satisfactory and in harmony with God's plan.

9

Forgiving: Healing Power

Anger and forgiving are intertwined. Many of our responses to anger are expressed in resentment, and resentment is rarely cleared up without forgiving.

Forgiving is something we do; forgiveness is something we receive. We use the word *forgiving* here to put the emphasis on our responsibility to take the initiative to forgive others.

When people hurt us, we must forgive them. It is a command in Jesus' own words: "When you stand praying, if you hold anything against anyone, forgive him, so that your Father in heaven may forgive you your sins" (Mark 11:25). This is no ordinary command —it is an ultimatum. The penalty if we do not obey is a failure to receive forgiveness from God. This should tell us all we need to know about the importance God places on forgiving. But see also Proverbs 25:21–22; Matthew 6:12–15; 18:21–35; Luke 6:37; 17:3; Romans 12:19.

Forgiving is an act of unselfishness, and unselfishness is the opposite of our natural human condition. We find it hard to forgive very much or very quickly. Often we feel that we can forgive only partially, but we are responsible to forgive others to whatever extent we can at the moment.

The Most Unselfish Act

The grandest expression of love is to forgive. It is our most unselfish act and therefore the most difficult and most rewarding.

Forgiving is like a railroad track that presses onward across the prairie. It will not be pushed aside by weeds of rationalization that grow up around it, and it will not be crushed by fear of vulnerability. Straight and purposeful it moves forward toward completion even though it may be a journey of great length.

The true forgiver does not wait until "feeling like it," but forgives immediately. Then the good feelings come: warmth created out of a willful intention to love others, and a sense of security arising from deliberate faithfulness to God's commands.

As we forgive, resentment is displaced by joy; barriers between people turn to bonds of trust; the blight of dislike heals, and friendship flowers; and sounds of suspicion turn to sounds of celebration. The way in which mismanagement of anger can complicate life, and the way in which forgiving can restore broken relationships, are shown in the experiences of Gayle, a Christian who discovered the healing power of forgiving.

Gayle wanted to be a good mother, and she worked hard at it. So hard, in fact, that her overconcern about her performance as a mother was part of what brought her to my counseling office. During several sessions in which we dealt with a number of issues, she began referring to "something that I need to talk with you about, but I'm not ready yet. It's too bad to tell you now." Several more sessions went by, and we talked about many things that were strongly emotional and deeply personal, but this other matter that she described as "too horrible to talk about" remained taboo. Obviously it was something that was important for us to deal with—but it had to be done at her timing.

Everything I knew about her then showed her as a very caring, gentle, loving person seeking to live as a Christian woman. She had a tendency though, to keep her feelings deep inside—the pattern of a person who might let anger build up and come out explosively. I wondered what she was holding back.

Finally the day came. It was apparent that she was ready to talk from the time she entered the office. She sat nervously in her chair and began speaking almost immediately.

"I want to talk about it," she said.

"And I want to hear about it," I responded.

"It was really awful," she said almost in a whisper. Her fingers clung to the arms of the chair; her chin and lips quivered. "I wanted to kill my son."

I was stunned by this revelation. Although I thought I was prepared for anything, this statement was so out of character with her deep Christian commitment and the quality of her life that I struggled to say, "I'm glad you are telling me about it. It must be very, very painful for you even now as you remember it."

"Yes, and I still can't believe I felt that way, but I did, and it was horrible."

We talked about the importance of discussing that impulse thoroughly now, about the need to understand and deal with what had caused it, and about the importance of resolving the problem. We talked of the opportunity for complete healing of the incident.

Then she told her story. Her son, age eleven, had been playing alone in the basement on a cold winter day many months before. Bored with indoor activities, he could hardly restrain himself when he found his baseball. How good it would feel, he thought, to be playing baseball again. He tossed the ball lightly from one hand to another a few times, and then boyish instincts took control—he threw the ball full force from one end of the basement to the other.

Upstairs, Gayle heard a loud noise from the basement. Coming down the stairs, she met her son on his way up. As they stood facing each other, he was trying his best to look casual and innocent. From the stairs she could see what had happened. The baseball had hit a large can of blue paint, knocking it from a shelf onto the top of the washing machine. The can had popped open on impact and a gallon of blue paint was flowing across the top of the washer, down the side, and across the floor. That's when she exploded.

She said, "I wanted to push him backward down the stairs. I wanted to kill him! I really wanted to kill him!"

"What did you do?" I asked.

"I screamed at him." She was trembling with shame. "I just yelled at him. I said 'Go to your room! Stay in your room, and don't come out until I say you can!' It was the worst moment of my life!"

"Then what?"

"Then I went down and cleaned up the mess. After

that I told him he could go over to one of his friends' homes, and I got busy fixing supper."

"Have you talked to him about it since then?"

"No, I'm just too ashamed. And I'm scared. I'm afraid I'll do something like that again. I'm afraid that I'm going to be a bad influence on him. I'm so ashamed. I'm his mother and I'm supposed to love him, but look how I acted."

Frankly I don't think Gayle did badly at all. Most parents of eleven-year-olds know that, while it may not be desirable, it's typical to have occasional moments of intense anger.

Right Actions

Moreover, Gayle did a couple of things right. For one, she separated the two of them so that matters did not get worse. Under the circumstances, that was a loving behavior after all. The other thing that she did right was to put her physical energy into something constructive—cleaning up the mess. Yes, it would have been better if he had cleaned up his own mess, but at this point Gayle was not capable of arranging that.

She did make a serious mistake in not resolving the matter with her son as soon as possible. This mistake signaled a deficiency in her that had contributed to her explosiveness. Further conversation with her revealed to me that she had been carrying unresolved anger toward her father, anger that was many years old.

Gayle needed to do two things. First, she had to clear up the incident with her son. She did this right away. She talked to him, apologized for her behavior, explained her love for him, and discovered that he felt a deep love for her and was not holding feelings of fear, resentment, or mistrust toward her. The apprehension and guilt that she had been feeling were unnecessary.

The second matter she had to deal with was her old resentment toward her father, an active man living nearby. Her father had frequently abused her, both physically and verbally, many years earlier. It did not seem appropriate for her to talk to him in specific terms about that now, so the two of us prayed together several times over a period of a few weeks. She also prayed regularly to be able to forgive him for his failures—some of which had been deliberate, but most of which had been due to ignorance or to his human shortcomings as a parent.

When Gayle forgave her father, she no longer had to be angry with him. That also freed her from the guilt she felt about her anger. It freed her from the condemnation she thought she was getting from her father. It freed her from feelings of unworthiness and from ideas about condemantion from her neighbors that had always been unrealistic but had inhibited and controlled her life. As she forgave, the resentment rolled away and lifted with it her enslavement to questions like "Will my neighbors think my house is clean enough?" and "Will my parents criticize my children?" and "Will the children do well enough in school?" It all seemed, to Gayle, too good to be true. It seemed like a miracle to her, and it was, but at its basis it was so simple: she followed God's principle that in loving, we are healed.

"The Odd Couple"

It is pleasing to describe these true examples of the power of forgiving, so I will include this story of a married couple. I thought of them as "the Odd Couple." If there were a hundred married couples in a room and we didn't know who was married to whom, we could match up ninety-nine couples correctly and have this husband and wife left over. They seemed obviously mismatched. We would be sure we had made a mistake—these two couldn't possibly belong together.

But together they had been, for fifteen years of flaming abusiveness. Physically they were well matched—each had bruised the other many times—and verbally their samples of vulgar profanity matched anything I had heard in a military barracks. They came wanting to save their marriage—what was left of it.

They were regularly involved in a church and said that their Christianity was important to them. One day, in an individual session with the husband, I quizzed him about his belief in prayer. He agreed that God hears our prayers and responds to them in ways that are best for us. But the couple had never prayed together. I suggested to him that they pray together regularly, if only briefly, on behalf of their marriage relationship. He thought it was a good idea.

Next week I saw her alone. They had not prayed. I asked her also about her beliefs and attitudes about prayer, and she said she believed in the power of prayer. But when I asked her, "What would you think about the two of you praying together on behalf of your marriage?" she bluntly retorted, "Oh, no! That would be too personal!"

I laughed. "Do you mean to tell me that you could call him [and I quoted a couple of her expletives] and *that* wouldn't be too personal but *praying* would be too personal?" She laughed, too, at the incongruity of it, but she didn't think praying together was possible.

So they argued about that for a couple of weeks, and then they came in again. Things had gone well.

"What caused this?"

They didn't know.

"Did you pray together?"

They had.

"Do you suppose that prayer had anything to do with things going better?"

"Yes, maybe it did," they said. "I guess God helped us to do better; He helped us live the way we ought to."

Painful Prayer

It had been painful for them to pray together—as it usually is for couples who have not done it—because praying on behalf of another person is an act of unselfishness. It is incompatible with a spirit of attack. It makes us vulnerable. It means not saying all the unkind things we might want to say. But this couple had tried it, and it had worked.

This husband and wife had piled up a lot of emotional garbage over the years, and that heap stood between them. No wonder they couldn't get close! They first declared a truce: No new fighting until the old junk was cleared away. It was a suspicious truce, but it was the best they were capable of, so God responded to that.

It takes God's help to clear up the old junk, and He doesn't help us do this so long as we're deliberately throwing new stuff on the pile. But as we begin exercising our own control over our behavior, the pile of old resentments begins to melt away.

The couple prayed off and on—some weeks regularly, other weeks not at all. Each time they came in, we talked briefly about it, and I wrote down in their words how much they had prayed and what effect it had.

After several months I pulled out all the notes, and we reviewed what had happened. It was clear: When they prayed, things went well; when they did not pray, things got worse. They were convinced that prayer works just the way the Bible says it will. They said, "With God's help, we can do it."

Sadly, however, the wife chose to file for divorce. She said, "Yes, we could have a good marriage if we wanted to. We've proved that. I just don't want to." Selfishness had won. In the end they agreed on just one thing—that the opportunity was there for them to have a good marriage. For them and for me, it was vivid proof of God's faithfulness to restore battered relationships. And I believe that if it could happen for the "Odd Couple," it could happen for anyone who wants restoration. God does not take away the freedom He has given us, and this includes the freedom to reject His goodness and mercy. The wife in this instance used that freedom to make a bad choice.

Productive Choices

In another example, an angry married man made more productive choices. Carl was forty-seven when I first met him. He described himself as "irritable all the time and explosive on a regular basis." He had grown up in a Christian home. His father, who owned a retail store, was a kind man with good intentions, but he was immersed in his work and did not spend time with his three children. The father was very athletic; he played and watched a lot of baseball, though never with Carl. So Carl got the message that for some reason, in some way, he was not good enough.

Carl described his mother as the dominant parent, an extremely critical woman who would dole out harsh and arbitrary punishment. One summer evening Carl was an hour and a half late for dinner, so for punishment he was not allowed to play with his friends for a week. He remembers pressing his face against the window screen in his second floor bedroom on those long summer evenings, listening to the sounds of his friends at play, brushing the tears from his cheeks, and wondering to himself, *What's wrong with me?*

After college Carl married someone very much like his mother and, sure enough, he couldn't please her either. They had been married for twenty-one years when I met Carl. He described the fights they had had, and I asked him how long they had been fighting like that. "Twenty two years," he replied. Carl began to recognize that, although he was successful in a management position, he was very uncomfortable with people generally and held a strong resentment toward all women, not just his wife.

Both of his parents were in their mid-seventies and still living when Carl and I got acquainted. That they had made mistakes as parents was obvious. That they had, however inadvertently, shown unloving attitudes and inflicted psychological pain on Carl certainly seemed to be the case. Clearly there were wounds for which Carl needed to forgive them, but to hold them fully responsible for the problems in Carl's life would not be appropriate.

In his own heart, and through prayer, Carl began to forgive his parents for the hurting things they had done and for the things they had failed to do. As this was accomplished, it became possible for him to fall in love with his wife for the first time. In this relationship there was also the need for forgiving on both sides, and as that forgiving has taken place, their resentments and fears have been displaced by joy and peace.

How to Forgive

Forgiving is required of the Christian. It benefits the person who forgives, and, as illustrated through true examples, when people forgive it makes a dramatic difference in their lives. It is useful for us to consider some practical suggestions concerning the process of forgiving.

Much has been written in Christian literature about the mystery of God's unlimited capacity to forgive us. However, relatively little is available that spells out in a practical, step-by-step way how we poor, finite humans can forgive others. That's the bad news. The good news is that everyone who has sought help from God in forgiving another person has found that help, and the forgiving has had tremendous impact. Forgiving is not so much something we need to be taught as it is something that we will be able to do as soon as we decide we want to. A few suggestions are listed here, because there are two obstacles to forgiving. The first is not expecting enough from ourselves and hence not trying to forgive; second is expecting too much too quickly.

There is only one place to begin. We must understand that the full forgiving of another person for his or her sins against us is possible only with God's assistance. Another basic understanding is that we do not forget these sins. Memories normally remain imprinted in our brains throughout life. However, the harmful effects of the incident that resulted in pain or fear, anger or anguish, despair or worthlessness need no longer influence us. Usually after forgiving, the factual part of memory remains but the emotional damage is neutralized. A third basic concept is that forgiving does not happen all at once; it is generally an on-going process in which we forgive to whatever extent we are capable at that point in time. As we grow capable of forgiving more completely—as new things happen, or as additional things come into our conscious memory—we forgive those.

Forgiving often goes through a sequence of stages as we increase in our desire to forgive others. We need dialogue with God through prayer throughout this process, just as we need this throughout all of life. Without prayer, these steps are unlikely to accomplish much.

1. We must decide that we are willing to want to forgive. That's not too much, is it? We begin where we *can* begin, and for many this is the first meager step. We are not forgiving at this point because we don't even want to forgive, but we believe that we should and we decide that we are willing to begin wanting to. Then we must actually begin to forgive.

2. We must quit hurting the other person. Forgiving is the opposite of retaliation, and we can't do both. If we have really chosen to forgive, we will quit doing the things that are contrary to forgiving.

Rehearsing Forgiving

3. Rehearsing the act of forgiving is another important step. We can rehearse the act of forgiving in our mind as we prayerfully picture and hear in our minds the way we want it to happen. Or, we can talk with a

friend about it, even practicing saying some of the things that we might say to the other person.

When we forgive in real life and follow the direction of the Holy Spirit at that moment, the things we say then may not be at all what we rehearsed. But the rehearsal can be very beneficial anyway for these reasons: first, we practice doing what we need to do; second, as we practice, we learn a lot about ourselves, our behavior, and the other person; third, we are likely to find our attitudes beginning to change.

4. After rehearsing, we should set up a time to talk with the other person, face-to-face if possible. When we talk, we should try to make the other person comfortable. Our showing anger would probably only raise his or her defensiveness, but we should show how the other's behavior has affected us. We must make some kind of statement about the offense for which we are forgiving, for without an offense there is nothing to forgive.

5. During our talk we must make an explicit statement of forgiveness. This is essential: sometime, some way, there has to be a straight-out message of "I forgive you." It doesn't have to be expressed in these exact words, but they are hard to beat for being quick and easy to understand. They may be hard for the other person to accept, but that is not our problem.

6. Listening is crucial. We must listen for cues as to whether we are exaggerating or minimizing our ideas of what has happened. We should listen for greater insight into our sins against the other person, and listen to what he or she has to say, thereby communicating our acceptance of the person in spite of not accepting the behavior.

7. We must explain why we want to forgive, affirming the other person as a person. The message must come through that "You as a person are worthwhile." If we cannot say this in our own words, with no strings attached, we are not really forgiving.

8. Finally, we must claim the closing of the incident. If it seems appropriate, we might offer a prayer with the other person. We can pray rejoicing that, through God's mercy, it is possible to forgive, and then pray asking that the wounds of relationships be healed. Once the situation is resolved, we should keep it closed and refuse to think about it anymore.

Surmounting Obstacles

I am well aware that many complications can arise. Other persons may not accept our forgiveness. Indeed, they may be incensed that we even want to talk about having been hurt by them. They may not be available to talk with, or they may refuse to talk with us. Nevertheless, the elements in the process suggested above often need to be included, and, as we seek God's direction, He will show us ways to surmount the obstacles.

The more we care about other persons and the more dependent we are on them, the more vulnerable we are to being hurt by them and having anger as one of our emotional responses. As a result, anger is prevalent within families. Forgiving should be commonplace within all close relationships, especially families.

10

Anger in the Family: A Dangerous House Guest

Ann, age ten, watched her teen-aged brother getting into his car. She yelled, "I'll tell Daddy as soon as he comes home," and turned to gaze at the roof of the house where her jumprope had been tossed. Rick slammed the door, backed quickly out of the driveway, and shot down the street with screeching, smoking tires. He smiled when he saw, in the rearview mirror, black tracks of rubber. In the house, eighteen-month-old Becky was jumping up and down in her crib, screaming. Mother couldn't come—she was spanking Jason for scribbling on the walls.

When dad got home mother snapped, "What a day! And half of it's your fault! I didn't want you to change jobs—it's making trouble for everyone!" Dad did not look at her but grumbled, "I need some peace and quiet. Keep everybody out of the family room!" He hid there behind the newspaper, with knotted stomach and dark thoughts.

Maybe four children don't live in your house, but anger probably does. If it doesn't live there, it is certain to visit. It's common, and it's normal. Beware the household that claims to be immune to anger, but also beware the damage this two-faced intruder can inflict.

Impact on Relationships

We feel anger only toward people who are important to us. Family members are especially important to us, because they can give or withhold the love that each of us needs. Thus we are more likely to feel angry toward family members than toward strangers, and feel it more intensely. Anger is a high level of involvement. It is an opposite of indifference. It has impact on relationships, leaving them better or worse, depending on how it is expressed.

Rick expressed his anger in rage as he blasted away from the house. The parents showed signs of the cancer of resentment. Ann was indignant about the injustice that had been done to her. Rage is a swarm of hornets that attacts directly, resentment is a colony of termites that undermines the structure, and indignation is a bulldog that, although dangerous, can protect the family.

Parents must learn and also teach their children how to deal with anger so it is not expressed in rage or resentment. Indignation, as we have defined it, is proper, and we should learn how to channel the energizing effects of anger into constructive activity that effectively opposes evil inside and outside the family.

Why do parents get angry? Consider some of the

pressures parents receive just from their parental roles. Many uncertainties can threaten, such as, Will my child get hurt or sick, or fail at school? Will my child be successful? Will my child live a meaningful Christian life? Will my child continue to love me? Receiving rejection may be part of being a parent. The rebellious testing out by adolescents as they experiment with self-sufficiency and individuality, or improper feelings of rejection, if a child does not like the same things we do, threaten parents. We often experience a sense of loss as children move out of the home, if the child cannot do what we hoped he or she could, or if there are sudden changes in lifestyle. And of course, the frustrations of time demands, financial burdens, and the general confusion of a complex lifestyle add to parental pressures.

Most parents face many other adult pressures, so when these conditions are aggravated, it is difficult to respond calmly without anger.

Anger in Children

Why do children get angry? They too face a variety of external pressures. They are dependent on others and physically unable to defend themselves, and therefore they may feel threatened. A child is sensitive to rejection and can even perceive being left with a baby sitter as rejection if that is not explained. Many things can create real frustration for the child, such as being nagged at, confusion, lack of consistency on the part of parents, not being able to keep up with siblings, boredom, or blocks to personal development (a teenager not being given increasing amounts of freedom and responsibility, for example). A loss, such as moving or the death of a pet, can affect a child as much as an adult.

In addition, children often receive real injustice, from both within and outside the family, about which they legitimately may respond with indignation. They may be squelched in their quest to develop as unique individuals who are different in some ways than either parent. They may be physically abused or punished out of proportion to an infraction. They may get beaten up on the way home from school, or teased or taunted or cheated. Punishment may be capricious, or inadequately explained so that it seems capricious. There may be psychological abuse by parents, peers, or teachers, such as embarrassing the child before his or her peers, using sarcasm or other put downs, or expressing a lack of confidence ("You can never do anything right").

These injustices reap two consequences: they give the child something that he or she can easily be angry about at the present, and they reduce self-esteem so that the child grows up being excessively vulnerable to responding with anger in the future. There is no justification for injustice in the home. "Do not exasperate your children," Paul writes in Ephesians 6:4.

Children's Techniques

Children learn to use tantrums or sullenness as a technique of power. It may be used as a deliberate manipulation. A talented teen I knew said angrily, "If I can't have the car, I won't practice my piano lesson." His parents fell for the ploy. He has been trying to manipulate other people for twenty-five years since then, and his life is a mess.

This technique may also be used to meet a legitimate

need, such as a need to be noticed. A first-grader who was virtually ignored at home in a family of eight pouted and grumbled at school. Her teacher responded by trying to cheer her up. "Oh, joy!" the little girl thought. "Attention at last!" She grumbled more, and the teacher tried harder. The girl had trained her teacher well!

Anger should never be used manipulatively. It's too dangerous. Some anger will come, and that's okay; but to encourage it is wrong. To use it for purposes of control is wrong.

We must avoid giving in to manipulative expressions of anger, for yielding to them rewards wrong behavior. Under this condition it is usually best to leave the room during a child's tantrum. When it has subsided, we can teach the child how to deserve and earn power and responsibility. We can tell the child we will ignore future manipulations—and then, of course, we must stick to this commitment.

Anger and many other activities, however, are used by children to test whether the parent still loves them. This is frequent and probably inevitable among teens, and it should not be punished. It is a time for us to pray for patience, to seek to understand the child's world, to teach about relationship, and to search creatively for activities that draw us closer without impeding the child's movement toward independence.

Anger is used as an expression of personal power or individuality. Rick threw Ann's jumprope on the roof to prove to himself he had power over her life, if not over his own. When he saw the tire marks, he felt even more powerful. It was an immature sense of power, but to him it was better than nothing.

The "Cure" Phase

The "cure" phase begins by our taking responsibility for how we feel. In our example, mother blamed dad's job change for her feelings, and that's unfair. Especially within the family, we should take responsibility for ourselves and for helping rather than blaming another person. Paul said, "Nobody should seek his own good, but the good of others" (1 Cor. 10:24). We should restore, in any way necessary, damage caused by us.

In the cure phase we seek to understand the causes of the anger and, if appropriate, to remove them. If the causes cannot be removed, we need to learn why not. If mother is indignant because Jason scribbles on the wall, Jason needs to change that behavior. If Rick is enraged because he is expected home by 10:30 tonight, he needs to learn how to replace rage with obedience.

We should seek to understand what lies beneath the anger and to identify primary feelings and the conditions that contribute to them. For example, Rick may be enraged because he is afraid that "everybody else will be staying out as long as they want to—they will make fun of me." Family conferences to learn the basic causes of anger and to teach about proper responses are desirable. Parents need to talk these things out with each other, to rehearse handling controversial issues, and above all, to pray together about such specific issues as well as praying generally about family life.

All of us must learn how to deal with anger in our families as part of the cure. As Christian parents we should avoid putting ourselves in a fatigued, irritable condition that weakens our self-control. We should not discipline or make decisions while angry.

We teach children how to respond to the stresses of life through our examples. We should also teach them the difference between rage and resentment, in contrast to indignation, and teach them how to respond properly to each. We need to be an image of God's love and corrective discipline before them and we need to be as consistent as possible. We should teach our children how to handle disappointment.

It is important that we teach a child to have realistic, attainable expectations in all areas of life. We should not equate being a good child with an absence of anger, and we must encourage a child to talk about anger that is already there. We can be most effective as parents when we have the greatest amount of information about our child. If we punish a child for the honest expression of anger, we may lose much information that we desparately need in order to be that child's servant-parent.

Children must be allowed to express their anger appropriately. We can provide physical outlets, such as constructive work or reasonable play. This is the child's "first aid." But we must not let the situation rest with that. Following up with discussion and teaching is important.

When anger cannot be expressed openly, it goes "underground." Jason scribbled on the walls because he was angry but afraid to protest directly. He intended to blame the scribbling on Becky, but his timing was off. Had he been taught how to deal constructively with angry feelings, it would have been better for everyone. It is easy to see how his retaliatory action created more hardship and division. Yet, his father was unavailable to teach him constructive responses. Therefore his style was to retreat from the family, express his anger by defacing walls, and give mother more frustration, and build barriers between family members.

Children are unable to control their emotions as an adult can, so we must not expect them to. They need to learn, though, the importance of experiencing emotions fully without being controlled by them. Rick drove away in a dangerous mental and physical state and, according to statistics, was ripe for an accident. He needs to know that. Father, silently steaming in the family room, is inviting the deterioration of his health. He also needs to consider whether or not he will continue that course. As feelings are expressed, there are opportunities to teach children to use the emotional side of their lives, which is fully as sacred as the cognitive side of life, effectively, spiritually, and in God's service. People remain strangers when they fail to express their emotions adequately.

Acting Their Age

It's okay to expect children to act their age if we know what is possible for a person that age. When Becky stood screaming in her crib, she was using mature behavior for her stage of development. We should not expect the impossible—God doesn't.

Controlling the environment to produce fewer frustrations is a valuable tool for ridding our families of unnecessary anger. This is especially useful with younger children. For example, we can maintain a fairly regular schedule, keep forbidden articles out of reach, and avoid presenting children with toys or tasks that are too advanced for their level of development.

Using physical restraint, if necessary, to prevent a child from hurting property, self, or others is a legitimate part of teaching self-control. Children need to learn limits. We can teach what the limits are in our families and enforce them consistently. The destructive forms of the expression of anger should not be permitted.

We must accept our children as worthwhile, giving reassurance through words and touch that they are valued, respected, loved. Help them to see their strengths, to learn from difficult situations, and to set new goals. Let us show our affection clearly.

The pattern of expressing anger that children choose depends initially on what they see modeled by parents. Have our children seen or heard their parents fighting? Probably, whether we know it or not. Solving an angry situation is a good time to teach children honesty in expression, openness to understanding the other's point of view, and forgiveness. It's also a good way to resolve the conflict. Have a huddle and explain, if nothing more, that mom and dad are confused about how to handle the problem but that they love each other and are trying to work it out. Pray together: it can build family unity.

Parents, we ought to be indignant! The world wants our children in hell and it has a million ways of making the trip there look attractive. God wants us fired up to use the energy of righteous anger to battle the enemy sin, for the sake of our children.

We must protest evil where we live, sweep the trash of immorality and violence from our stores and streets, prod lawmakers and law enforces to action, care about one another, pray for the enemies of decency, rouse the parents and Chrsitians who practice the form of child abuse known as indifference, and support schools, churches, and institutions that teach God's truth.

We must allow ourselves to be shocked into feelings of anger and to channel that emotional/physical charge into vigorous action to oppose evil. God wants us holy, and He wants the world holy. He has given us part of His own capacity for charged up indignant action as one of His means of changing the world where we live. What are we going to do about it?

11

The Prevention of Anger

Is it possible to avoid all anger? Not really. But much anger is unnecessary and could be avoided. There are at least four good reasons for avoiding anger.

First, the Bible advises it. "Do not be quickly provoked in your spirit, for anger resides in the lap of fools" (Eccl. 7:9). "Better a patient man than a warrior, a man who controls his temper than one who takes a city" (Prov. 16:32). "Like a city whose walls are broken down is a man who lacks self-control" (Prov. 25:28). "Starting a quarrel is like breaching a dam; so drop the matter before a dispute breaks out" (Prov. 17:14). "A man's wisdom gives him patience; it is to his glory to overlook an offense" (Prov. 19:11). "Refrain from anger and turn from wrath; do not fret—it leads only to evil" (Ps. 37:8). The Bible cautions against anger because anger can devour us and eat us alive, from the outside or from the inside. Unless we learn to deal with it with confidence, anger is dangerous.

A second reason for avoiding anger is the serious effect of the physiological arousal caused by it. The heart rate accelerates, often close to its maximum; stomach and bowels tense up, interrupting digestion; blood pressure increases; and the lungs work more actively. Nothing can take place in the body without its affecting everything else about us. It is unquestionably true that our state of mind determines, in a very real sense, our state of body.

Potential for Destruction

Put simply, under unnecessary emotional stress, the body wears out more quickly than it needs to. Almost everything written on anger speaks of the tremendous potential for extreme physical destruction. Most lists of anger-related damage include hypertension and heart disease, stroke, ulcerative colitis, crippling arthritis, and suicidal depression. Anger—especially stifled anger—gets blamed for these things almost universally. The list could go on and on, depending on what authors are cited, but let us summarize the medical literature on the damage caused by anger in this way: it is clear that the damage can be intense and irreversible. It is irresponsible for the Christian to let this happen. We must be responsible stewards of our bodies, because it is through the use of our physical selves that we are able to serve God here on earth. We must protect ourselves and use our physical and emotional resources wisely.

Third, we can lose the opportunity to witness to our faith if we don't avoid anger. On one occasion, I almost allowed my anger to control me and to display a very unchristian message. A salesman was going to take me out to lunch, but he was already ten minutes late. I didn't have much time to spare, and now he was using up what I had. I felt annoyed. I drummed my fingers impatiently on my desktop and shuffled papers, and soon the salesman was fifteen minutes overdue. My irritation grew. A phone call to his office produced nothing: they didn't know where he was, and sarcastically I thought, "That's some way to run a business." I decided that if it got to be twenty minutes late, I would chew him out. I imagined myself saying, "Other salesmen get here on time—why can't you?"

When he arrived, I was ready to explode. But before I could speak, he said, "Sorry I'm late. I had to take my wife back to the hospital." He named a state psychiatric hospital. "She had been there for two years," he explained, "and finally came home a week ago. We were really happy about that. Then last night things got bad again, and about midnight I had to take her back. There wasn't any choice."

His words reverberated through my mind: "There wasn't any choice." No, for him there hadn't been; for me there was. There was the choice of whether to think about his major needs or my little ones. You see, there were many small occurrences that fed the feeling of time pressure and made it easy for that feeling of pressure to move toward feelings of anger and from there to the possibility of very destructive behavior. How close I had come to further wounding a man already deeply in pain! And close to spoiling, possibly forever, any chance for effective ministry for Christ!

The fourth reason for avoiding anger is that it interferes with our own lives. Rage will break communication with others and can easily lead to wrong behavior. Stuffing our anger inside isn't good, because it takes so much effort to keep it there. This saps emotional energy that could be used in having fun or doing constructive things. Even a small amount of smoldering resentment creates a barrier between persons and diminishes the joy of living.

Major Problems

But how do we prevent anger? Here are three major problems to work on and some practical suggestions within each.

1. We must clean up the old messes. Resolving past anger takes the yeast away so that the angry incidents do not remain as a starter for new anger. Part of cleaning up the old messes may be restitution. There is great preventive value in restitution, for the act of restitution both punishes us for our misdeed and rewards us for our courageous and unselfish obedience.

Do not let anger accumulate. Cleaning up the old mess means evaluating our internal conditions for symptoms of guilt, sense of helplessness, unrealistic expectations, and aimlessness. To make significant changes in any of these areas is usually not an instant event. But changes do need to occur; we must eliminate guilt. If we confess and repent, we will receive forgiveness from God for our sins.

Recall that a sense of helplessness may come from deficient self-esteem or from a lack of suppport from other persons. Our self-esteem will not be adequate as long as an awareness of guilt remains, but an appropriate amount of self-esteem is necessary for a healthy personality. The growth of self-esteem is usually a long process, and often the help of a professional counselor is needed. Building self-esteem begins with our refusing to injure ourselves by continuing to sin, by learning that we are valuable by virtue of being created in God's image, and by recognizing that we do not have to be perfect. It grows as we have more experiences of success, receive affirmation from others, and learn to celebrate being us.

We each need to have other persons in our lives who will listen, counsel, be with us quietly when we need that, who will seek to understand us, affirm, or admonish. We also need other persons for fun and sharing and variety. This will probably not happen unless we take the initiative to develop friendships at work, in the neighborhood, at church, and within the family. And, of course, a relationship with God and knowing the comfort and counsel of the Holy Spirit is most meaningful of all.

Our expectations must be realistic. This means bringing our love for ourselves to a healthy point so that we can relate with other persons as servant friends, not as conqueror to subject; as colleagues, not as superstar to klutz. This happens as we begin to understand the sinful nature of pride and the expression of pride in selfishness, arrogance, and indifference to the needs of others. Again, these attitudes and behavioral habits can be so ingrained that it may well require the assistance of a strong outside person to help us understand and change this condition.

Finally we must learn to see our life as a whole in order to eliminate aimlessness. Discovering what is really important to us, clarifying our values, and knowing where we are going in life are part of this process. Aimlessness will change as we discover and accept purpose in life compatible with God's order. A systematic devotional life focused on learning God's order for Christians generally and for us specifically is helpful, as is the guidance of another person. Practicing positive living by taking responsibility for the quality of our lives, rather than by taking inactive or reactive response, is essential. Anticipate normal life-stress events such as marriage, the children's leaving home, or retirement and plan for a smooth transition into the new pattern of living. Learn to manage your time, money, and other resources so that they produce satisfaction instead of frustration.

Christian Maturity

2. We must become stronger, more mature Christians. This does not happen all at once.

Jesus chose as disciples the brothers James and John, "the Sons of Thunder" (Mark 3:17) or, in a more literal translation, "the Soon-angry Ones." Our common image of John, Jesus' favorite disciple, is that of a peaceful, loving person, but there was another side to him. He abruptly interrupted Christ's discourse on humility (Luke 9:46–50), demanded fire to consume a Samaritan village (Luke 9:51–56), plotted behind the back of the other disciples for power in Christ's kingdom (Mark 10:35–40). As a result of John's attitudes and behaviors, Jesus and the other disciples showed anger (Luke 9:55; Mark 10:41).

John changed. Between the time that we see him as an impetuous, self-seeking disciple and as a saintly writer, John's attitudes and behaviors were transformed. His selfish ambition was displaced by a devotion to the principles Christ had taught, a devotion expressed in dedicated servanthood. We should seek to change in the same way, but it took time for John and it will for us. Following are some specific suggestions about this process:

We must seek to develop spiritual strength. Christian living helps us become less selfish, more tolerant, and therefore less likely to evoke the anger of others. As we grow we learn to be more flexible with others, giving in where possible instead of insisting on our way.

As Christians we are to treat all persons as worthwhile, even though their behavior may be wrong, ugly, and disgusting. Certainly this was the pattern of Christ's ministry. Consider His compassion for persons whose behavior was wrong and who were despised by the general public. Read about his dealing with the adultress (John 8:1–11); with Nicodemus (John 3:1–21), and with the Samaritan woman at the well (John 4:4–42). The model of relationship given us by Christ is one combining caring and confrontation. He loved people, but denounced their sins.

Unlike Christ, we as sinful creatures must work hard to be interested in other persons. But when we become "Quick to listen, slow to speak," we will also develop the quality of being "slow to become angry" (James 1:19). By keeping open the lines of communication, we will learn to see the other person's point of view and be less readily judgmental.

Another aspect of open communication means reporting our initial bad feelings to others concerned, rather than waiting for those feelings to generate anger. For example, "I need to be listened to. When you don't, I feel rejected. That hurts." After such a report the other person may apologize or change, which rewards you for your effort. He or she is unlikely to react harshly to this approach. Chapter 14 offers more instructions in this regard.

Emotional Overload

3. When we feel anger coming on, we must remind ourselves that anger is okay and that we are not going to do wrong. We must be moderate in behavior, not letting our emotional system get overloaded. Then we can congratulate ourselves for good sense and self-control. If we know the first-aid control methods, it will increase our confidence; we will feel less threatened by the possibility of losing control of our anger.

4. Stay in good physical shape. Exercise, fun, good diet, and rest build tolerance to stress.

5. Also remember to defuse anger early and to nip conditions in the bud. Practice the first-aid methods suggested in chapter 7.

6. Finally we can learn to evaluate our lives in order to understand how pressure builds in us. Learn what increases pressure and what relieves pressure and brings satisfaction. This understanding of cause and effect is important, but far more important is our conscious, intentional commitment not to be controlled by anger and to experience the feelings that come, being guided by belief in God's order for the world.

Flirting With Trouble

Once we have evaluated what situations increase pressure in our lives, we can learn to walk around trouble. We will be treating ourselves with a lot more respect when we avoid uncomfortable situations than when we carelessly let ourselves get worked up with an unpleasant emotion like anger. Sometimes we need to face a problem and defeat it, but we should know what we are doing—flirting with trouble or staring it down.

We can avoid contact with people, situations, and activities that are likely to result in anger until we develop the confidence and tolerance to handle them. For example, stay off that street with the sticky traffic or stay out of the store with the rude clerks. Moreover, developing our sense of humor and cultivating optimism can help us learn to laugh at these routine hassles of life.

Use the suggestions in chapter 8 about an anger inventory. Make a list of situations that are likely to arouse anger in you. We must be prepared, knowing in advance how we will deal with a situation. Seek God's direction in understanding and eliminating the basic cause of these situations. During our evaluation we may learn that some of our habits need to be changed. If this is so, we must "do away with all the impurities and bad habits that are still left in you—accept and submit to the word which has been planted in you and can save your souls" (James 1:21, JERUSALEM BIBLE).

12

Anger Toward God

Sometimes all the prevention techniques in the world can't keep us away from situations that lead to anger. I can't prevent a car accident that kills my friend or prevent a flood that destroys my house. I can rant and rave about poor driving or bad weather, but when it comes right down to it, I know God could have kept those things from happening if He had wanted—but He didn't. Then I feel hurt and frustrated and afraid, feelings that easily may lead to anger. That anger may then be directed at God.

That's right, angry at God. When it seems that all His promises to me have gone up in smoke, it is difficult for me to relate to Him as a loving heavenly Father. Yet, do I have a right to feel angry toward God? Does the Bible ever say anger with God is wrong? The following observations, based on Scripture, form a basis for answering these questions.

This chapter was written in part by Miriam McNair Engler.

The Bible certainly says that not believing in God is sin. Not praying to Him is sin. Not being honest with Him is sin. Scripture says that it is sinful to lie to God about our relationship with Him or to stop talking to God (as though to punish Him) by not praying.

People, including Christians, do get angry with God when they experience great hurt. This is seen in several scriptural accounts. Job, a prominent Old Testament character, is certainly a prime example of a godly man who experienced deep hurt and who, as many suffering people do, felt angry. His anger was obvious to Bildad (Job 18:4), and we may reasonably assume that Job was feeling angry toward God when he said such things as, "I cry out to you, O God, but you do not answer; I stand up, but you merely look at me. You turn on me ruthlessly; with the might of your hand you attack me" (Job 30:20–21). God called Job a "perfect man" many times. God understood, accepted, and did not punish Job's blunt expression of angry despair.

Jonah disagreed vehemently with God's decision to spare Nineveh, and he reported his anger, saying, "I am angry enough to die" (Jonah 4:9). God's response to Jonah's anger was to teach him, not punish him.

David, emotionally vigorous all his life, prayed about his anger frequently: "Why, O LORD, do you stand far off? Why do you hide yourself in times of trouble?" (Ps. 10:1). "How long, O LORD? Will you forget me forever? How long will you hide your face from me?" (Ps. 13:1).

A Faithful God

We are not told that Elijah felt angry toward God, but we might suspect that he was, while living through some very trying circumstances. Jezebel wanted to kill him, so he fled to the desert and prayed that he might die. Afterward God provided food, and Elijah fled to the mountains for forty days and forty nights. Then this conversation took place: God said, "What are you doing here, Elijah?" And Elijah replied, "I have been very zealous for the LORD God Almighty. The Israelites have rejected your covenant, broken down your altars, and put your prophets to death with the sword. I am the only one left, and now they are trying to kill me too" (1 Kings 19:9–10). God, of course, remained faithful to Elijah, who was still zealous for the Lord—confused, afraid, and angry, but still obedient and believing.

When these godly men prayed, they were often recounting the belief they had in God's character. They did not understand the application of God's actions to their particular situation right then, but they said, "You are this kind of God." These men were following biblical principles concerning anger—dealing honestly, directly, and immediately with the person with whom they were angry.

So it seems acceptable to express honestly to God how we feel about Him even when the feeling is anger. The examples of these men show that. Other scriptural passages indicate God's love for us as we are, not as we think we should be.

The more important someone is in our life, the more likely we are to feel anger toward him or her? Have you ever felt angry toward Elmo X. Schwartz, Route 5, Buffalo Springs, Nebraska? No, because you don't know him. Have you ever felt angry toward your parents? Yes.

God is important to us because we were created with dependence on Him. Therefore it probably is inevitable that we will become angry with Him occasionally. He understands that and loves us unconditionally anyway.

Why is it important to express our anger toward God? Why not just condemn ourselves for our apparent lack of faith and be still? Because by doing this we are violating the very essence of salvation—it is God's power that can save us (Eph. 2:8–9) and not something we can do ourselves. He is able to deal with our feelings of anger toward Him and change them. In our own strength we are able only to be controlled by them, allowing them expression either in rage or resentment; and in either case they weaken our living vital relationship with Him because we are not being honest with Him.

Learning About God's Love

By expressing our anger openly and honestly toward God, we begin to learn how much vaster, firmer, and steadier God's love is than we ever knew before. We learn that He is powerful enough to change feelings as well as actions. We learn how dependable and never-changing He is. We learn that His love is limitless as he refines us and makes us holy as we begin to live in complete dependence on Him. Aren't these benefits reason enough to be honest with God? Shouldn't we let Him work in our lives rather than futilely try to pull ourselves up by our bootstraps?

Does this mean, however, that we should unleash all feelings we have toward God defiantly—throwing our animosities at Him? No, for that would be rebellion, the flaunting of our independence from Him, placing ourselves above Him. We may rest confidently in His total love for us, but He demands obedience, respect, and submission of our will to His. We are to report our feelings and cooperate, not compete; then we can learn from God, rather than foolishly try to teach Him.

Limitations to Anger

There are some dangers in telling God we are angry with Him. The same limitations apply to being angry with God as pertain to expressing anger toward our brothers.

The first limitation is that for any relationship to grow by dealing with angry feelings, both parties must be speaking and listening. There are many biblical examples of men angrily telling God off and then refusing to listen to Him in His response. Job listened, as did Jonah, Elijah, and David. They realized that God was bigger than their feelings, and that their feelings were only their own perspective on the matter. So they listened to God to get His perspective.

"Great," you say. "I'm willing, but how do I listen to God? He spoke directly to Job and Jonah and maybe he wants to communicate with me, but sometimes it seems as if he doesn't say much to me." Today God usually chooses means other than an audible voice to speak to us. He is not limited to human ways of speaking. God is more than capable of getting a message across if we are open to hearing it. He speaks through His written Word, the Bible. He often speaks through other Christians who are living their lives in godly ways, through preaching and teaching, and He reveals Himself individually in the unfolding patterns of our personal lives. If we want to hear God, we can.

The second limitation to our anger is the biblical principle that we must deal directly with the person with whom we are angry—in this case, God. This requires us not to blame other people or situations when we believe God is responsible. God makes it clear that anger is to be dealt with, not allowed to grow and fester into bitterness. Deep hurt often requires us to come to God daily or hourly with anger and bitterness. A decision of the will to bring these feelings to God as often as necessary does not mean that we are dwelling in anger, but is an act of faith that God wants to heal us and will heal us in His own time.

The third limitation on our expression of anger toward God comes from His commands about vengeance. Never are we given the right to "get even" when we have been hurt. Never are we given the right to curse God in our anger toward Him or to reject God because of our hurt.

A Vital Difference

But what is the difference between talking angrily to God and cursing Him? Are they not essentially the same? No, and the difference between them is actually the foundation for our having an honest relationship with God. Cursing God is saying "I'm angry with you and I'm going to hurt you, blame you, and break my relationship with you because I don't believe you are the God you claim to be." This is rebellion, and it is sin.

We should not, in our anger, reject God. There is a vital difference between reporting to God our feelings of frustration and disappointment, and defying His power or rejecting His love. The latter would be both wrong and foolish. We would be competing with God in a futile attempt to usurp His place, and this is the basis of all sin.

Expressing existing anger with God should have a motivation and purpose directly opposite from cursing, rejecting, or defying Him. The angry Christian might pray, for example, "I am deeply hurt. I don't understand why things are the way they are, and I don't like it. You seem to be ignoring me, and I feel unloved, rejected, and angry. I'm telling You, because I believe that You love me and care about how much I hurt even if it doesn't feel like it right now." This is reporting what already exists and is seeking restoration and healing in relationship to God, rather than brokenness and independence. This kind of honesty and trust pleases God. Not to report what exists is to pretend that we can fool God, and that is itself a passive form of rebellion.

Restoration and healing are always the biblical objective of expressing anger, whether with a brother or with God. It requires a lot of faith to believe God is still there and still cares when hurts go deep. It also takes a lot of faith to believe He loves us enough to accept our anger and can even work through that anger to teach us more about Him and to shape us more completely into His image.

A Sign of Trust

If we have anger toward God, telling Him about it is a way of showing Him that He is important to us. Reporting our inner experience and our feelings to God indicates trust. We don't trust someone unless we believe that he or she will act in our behalf. Talking to God gives Him another way of showing us that He loves us.

It was through talking about my anger to God that I reached a new plateau in understanding His love for me. It happened during a period of time in which I was working hard to understand Him better and to understand how to live as a useful Christian, but I felt that God was not listening to me. At this time the deadline for a big vocational decision was quickly approaching. I was asking God for counsel and not hearing it. I felt rebuffed and angry by the lack of response from God but I didn't want God to find out how I felt. So I prayed earnest but safe prayers, careful to delete my actual feelings and attitudes. How foolish it is to pretend we can keep secrets from God who knows everything!

Finally, in my desperation, I prayed the truth: "God, it seems as if You've gone off and left me. I keep talking to You, but You don't talk back, You don't make anything happen. You must not even care about me any more, if You ever did and if You're even listening to me now. This is how I feel. I wish I didn't, but I do. Please answer me."

While praying, I was somewhat disinterested, thinking that maybe God really didn't care and maybe He wasn't out there anyway. I was also afraid, expecting to be struck by lightning right there in my home. I paused for a moment, expecting something to happen, and when it didn't, I trudged off to work.

This incident reveals a lot about the immaturity of my Christianity at that point and my incomplete understanding of God's love. In the prayer, I was honest with God, and He responded by vividly showing me His love for me. During that same day, things happened. A nice sum of unexpected money came in the mail, my brother-in-law from two hundred miles away strolled into my office, and my brother phoned to chat. By the end of the day, these and six other special and happy events had occurred.

Now don't think for a minute that a tantrum will get us what we want. Not at all. The way I look at this is that God showed me that He was in control all along. The lesson God taught was, "You can trust me with all of your being. You don't have to hold back the angry part of you in fear that I will hurt you." He showed me this with a clear object lesson, because I was too shortsighted to learn by any less dramatic means. In my case, when God taught me about His love, it involved my disclosing my anger to Him. The way in which God teaches you about His love may be quite different, so if you have occasion to disclose your anger toward God to Him, the style of His response may be quite different. Rest assured that it will be right for you.

As our maturity level increases, we become more capable of learning without the dramatic object lessons, and more responsible in using our beliefs and faith. We must not have tantrums, expecting God to shower us with good things to appease us—this would be quite wrong, because we would be trying to manipulate God. On the other hand, we must understand that God loves us in spite of any and all fears about Him we may have, and in spite of resentments or anger that we have toward Him because of those fears or misunderstanding. Being honest with God gives Him a chance to be more honest with us, and His honesty with us is the best thing that can happen in our lives.

What we learn from God's style of response to our anger will help us when we have occasion to respond to other people when they are angry.

13

When the Other Person Is Angry

There are many angry people around us. It is a symptom of the complex and uncertain times in which we live. We may not become angry often ourselves, but it is certain that angry persons will frequently come into our lives.

God does not avoid the angry person. "Once you were alienated from God and were enemies in your minds because of your evil behavior. But now he has reconciled you . . ." (Col. 1:21–22). We should follow the pattern suggested in these verses, sensibly reaching out to the angry in spite of their hostile, offensive behavior.

The style with which we normally speak and act toward another person needs to be modified when that person is angry. The situation can be kept under control if we respond properly, in a way that takes into consideration the barriers to good communication that result from their feelings.

The first thing that needs to be examined is whether or not we are responsible for having caused the anger. If the anger is justifiable and is in response to our wrongs against him or her, we must admit it fully and willingly. For example, "Well, of course you are angry—I said I would do that by now, and I haven't!" No alternative will be as effective in the long run. Taking responsibility will probably include apologizing and doing all that we can to restore conditions to what they were. If we can let the angry person know that something can be done about the problem, we should say so at once.

Wrong Responses

There are always many ways to do anything wrong, and that is true of responding to an angry person. In fact, since anger is so contagious, we often react with anger, and it is very easy for us to respond ineffectively. It is useful to look at the ineffective styles, which are likely to produce only more anger in the already irate person. These styles are often used by weak persons trying to appear strong. In the following situation see whether you recognize a style that you yourself have used.

The angry person is president of a community organization and is talking with the treasurer of the group. We will assume both are men. The president says loudly, "I need to talk to you right now! This is terrible! Look at the bank book—we're overdrawn! What are you trying to do, you turkey—get us thrown in jail?"

The treasurer can respond in five different ways, each of them ineffective.

1. The "delay" ineffective style is said in a condes-

cending, "holier than thou" manner: "Well, if you want to talk about it, we can do that, but not now while you're so upset and unreasonable. You aren't even talking sense. If you will settle down and act civilized, *then* we'll talk about it."

In this style the treasurer is telling the president that he will not talk until the other quits being angry. The most likely effect is that the angry person gets angrier because this makes the relationship conditional. He feels criticized and somewhat rejected, which only fuels his anger. The request to quit being upset is unreasonable, for he probably would already have quit being angry if that were possible. Such comments as "Calm down, will you?" and "Get yourself together, you're acting like a baby!" are condescending and do not accept the other person as worthwhile even though his behavior may be obnoxious at the moment. It is like telling a bursting balloon to pull itself together.

This ineffective way of responding to an angry person is totally different from God's style with us. God has not told us to go out and get our act together before we can come to Him.

2. The "oblivious" ineffective style doesn't use any words at all; the president is met with a blank, disinterested expression and then ignored. Being ignored is probably the most emotionally devastating thing that can happen to us. It is the supreme insult because it says, "You do not exist." Anger is often used to get attention, so this kind of response further angers the other person. The angry person is likely to fight harder, make more noise, and utter stronger insults in order to get attention.

Nevertheless, when anger is being expressed manipulatively, it is proper to ignore it. There is further comment about this later.

3. The "rational" ineffective style has an "I'm smart, you're stupid" tone of voice: "You don't understand. We're not really overdrawn—it only looks that way on paper. What I've done is to allow for the processing time. I know for a fact that those two biggest checks won't get back to our bank for at least a week. We've got plenty of 'float time.' This is something I've done for years, so don't worry about it. Besides, they don't put people in jail for a simple little thing like this."

The information given in this "rational" response may be valid and useful information, but can the president use it right now? A person full of anger probably doesn't have room for reason. Logical, rational explanations cannot begin to flow in until the anger has flowed out. The most likely result, therefore, is that the president does not hear the treasurer's explanations accurately, and they are wasted—or he hears but wants to argue. Arguing is a waste of time. Dale Carnegie said, "The only way to win an argument is to avoid it." Your goal should be to bring both of you into dialogue; pursue constructive debate, not competitive argument.

4. The "analytical" style also has a condescending manner: "You are blowing this all out of proportion because of your own doubts and conflicts. You are projecting your hostilities on me as a defense mechanism and, though the catharsis may help you feel better, ultimately you need to resolve the root causes that go back to mishandling of sibling rivalry as a child." The only thing worse than an expert is a person who thinks he is. Few things make other persons more angry than playing "amateur psychologist" with them. The

analysis might even be accurate, but plain old under-standing would be much more beneficial.

5. The "fiery" response involves as much screaming and jumping up and down as the angry president used: "If I'm a turkey you're a goose, so waddle off and honk in someone else's ear! What you're doing now is stupid! I call the financial shots, and I don't need you butting in! You should work as hard at your job as you do in second-guessing mine! So buzz off!"

This is justified as an extension of the "fight fire with fire" principle, but it is actually an excuse for indulging one's own anger immaturely. It doesn't help; it only causes the conflict to grow. And it contradicts Proverbs 26:20–21: "Without wood a fire goes out; . . . as wood to fire, so is a quarrelsome man for kindling strife."

Generally we receive in kind from others what we give. If we give anger, especially to an angry person, we will get more anger in return. As Christians we are able, if we choose, to rise above the simple "eye for an eye, tooth for a tooth" retaliation.

Effective Sequence

Each of these ineffective responses rejects the angry person, which adds to his discomfort. We need a re-sponse style that meets scriptural injunctions to "over-come evil with good" (Rom. 12:21). Here is a sequence that meets biblical criteria:

1. We seek to show acceptance of him or her as a person and a willingness to understand the issues and causes of the anger;

2. "First aid" helps the angry person to calm down physiologically;

3. Through dialogue we both understand the angry

person's feelings and the causes of the anger;

4. The appropriate person or persons takes constructive action.

This sequence holds the greatest probability of eliciting reasonable behavior from the other person. Let us consider each of the steps in detail.

1. *Show acceptance.* The first approach is to seek to communicate acceptance of the person and willingness to understand his or her behavior. The treasurer in our example might have responded like this: "You show a lot of concern about how things are being handled. I'll try to explain what you want to know about the club money. Do you want to talk about it right now?" This shows acceptance of the president even though he was angry at the time and this is very unpleasant. Basically, he is giving the message, "It's okay for you to express your anger. I will take it seriously." That message says, "I like you." It is a simple message but, because anger may get us uptight when we are around it, it can sometimes be hard for us to give even this simple message.

Nonverbal Elements

Both the words and the nonverbal elements are important. An angry person tends to see and hear things in an exaggerated way because of the "fight or flee" physical changes, so whatever we say should be clear, brief, and sincere.

A nonverbal response can help the angry person cool down. Our style should be low key. We should speak a little more slowly and quietly than usual. "A gentle answer turns away wrath, but a harsh word stirs up anger" (Prov. 15:1). Keep the body relaxed, avoiding dramatic gestures and moving less and more slowly than usual. Eye contact should be direct and steady. Posture should be relaxed, but attentive; the distance between us and the angry person should not be as close as usual.

Let the angry person talk. Most people cooperate with us when they believe we are trying to provide what they want. They will respond positively and reasonably when treated with respect and cooperation. What we do affects the other person's attitude and behavior toward us.

Our goal is to help the person get relief from the pressure of angry feelings. Let him or her spout off harmlessly. When anger is allowed to flow unchecked from the other person, it will soon dissipate. Spouting off helps the angry person feel worthwhile and builds feelings of trust. Permitting him or her to talk helps us earn the right to be heard. However, this is only a preliminary step; communication and constructive action begin after the anger is vented. We should not say anything or give a nonverbal expression that the other person can interpret as criticism of his or her words or actions.

When anger flows away, trust and caring, which are the basis for friendship, can begin. Don't be surprised if the first reaction of the angry person is disbelief. We may be the first person who has responded to the anger by treating him or her with acceptance and dignity.

Communicating Acceptance

Here are some suggestions to help us accept a person who is expressing anger:

We can pray within our hearts.

We can be confident that we will come through the

situation successfully, reminding ourselves that it is our intention not to make matters worse, and that we have been learning recently about how to control our own angry feelings. With our intention and skills, we are prepared.

We should realize that the angry person has given up a lot of control over what he or she is saying and has a tendency to exaggerate to get attention. A lot of what we are hearing should be ignored.

We must remember that anger is usually a secondary emotion. In all probability there is pain that we do not know about in the angry person's life. Let us pause to realize that if we knew about those things, it would be easier to have different feelings about the person.

2. *Apply "first aid."* Angry people need "first-aid" measures because their perception is likely to be distorted while they are angry. They need to settle down to a state of mind from which they can move toward resolving the problem. The acceptance and willingness to understand them that we have already shown verbally and nonverbally is the most important part of this.

We can also agree with and affirm whatever we can, even seeking things about which we can agree. We might change the subject temporarily and, if appropriate, we should assure the angry person of our respect and caring, for he or she is likely to be uneasy about that while expressing anger. We should continue to make it clear that we are interested in helping him or her, in any way we can, to improve the circumstances.

3. *Work toward understanding.* Listen. Try to understand an angry person's point of view. If we are not willing to do this, we ourselves don't deserve to be heard. Moreover, if we haven't listened to the angry

person, our suggestions are not likely to be very accurate or relevant.

As we gain more information, we must check again to determine whether we have contributed to the cause of the anger. As we listen, we can pray for discernment to see our part of the problem, if any; for courage to take responsibility for our part; and for wisdom to either help the person or to keep quiet, whichever is in that person's best interest.

4. *Constructive action.* The other person may need to do some of the "cure" activities that we have used. Our experience and counsel may be helpful. But we should not take responsibility that they should accept.

What to Avoid

There are, of course, exceptions to this sequence. In some situations the usual guidelines don't apply. It is important to be prepared for this also. There are times when we should avoid the angry person. We should be very cautious with angry strangers. In this age of sudden violence, we must size up the risk carefully. Know when to say, casually, something like "I'm not interested in pursuing this" and quietly leave. It can also be impractical to respond to anger if your boss is angry and unproductive if the expression of anger concerns something trivial. Assess the potential for helping the person, and if there isn't any prospect of benefit, leave the situation alone.

Second, when anger is used manipulatively, the usual steps are difficult to follow. Anger can be expressed deliberately for several reasons. It may be an immature way of showing strength or individuality or coercing others into cooperation. It may be used as a defensive maneuver to keep people away or as a method to get close to others. Anger may also be used deliberately to relieve boredom, to bring on punishment, or to release tension. These are immature or pathological conditions and should not be rewarded.

We should tell the person in advance that we are unwilling to be controlled by manipulative angry behavior and that in the future we will ignore such demonstrations. If such behavior continues, its inappropriateness must be dealt with.

Finally, when anger is denied, we will have to handle it differently in different situations. When we are quite sure the other person is angry, but he or she won't admit it, we should try to make it easy for that person to talk about it. We might take the initiative by reporting our own feelings to them, such as, "I'm puzzled by how we're getting along lately. It seems to be going downhill. I'm wondering if I have done something to offend you. If that's happened, I'd like to know about it so I can do whatever I can to improve things." This lets the person know that it is safe for him or her to express anger to us. We can also give him or her permission to express anger by admitting our own present anger, if we have any, or by alluding to the fact that we sometimes do feel angry.

Responding to angry people is a challenge because of the intensity and unpredictability of their behavior. But the anger is a symptom of needs, and needs are opportunities to help someone and to share the love that God has shared with us. We can respond to the angry person, confident in the knowledge that as we seek to be God's servant, He will support us with the wisdom and courage that we need.

14

The Benefits of Anger

"Can a feeling as uncomfortable and dangerous as anger be beneficial?" we might ask. Yes, it can. It can even be an asset to the Christian, though most of us have not used it well.

The feeling of anger has two major benefits. First, it is a warning that something is wrong. It is a signal, like a headache, that alerts us to the existence of an underlying problem. The sensible person takes the warning seriously, seeks out the problem, and takes responsibility for resolving it to the extent possible.

A second benefit of the feeling of anger is that it can activate us to be involved with life. We get charged up emotionally and mentally. Anger triggers physiological processes that mobilize the body for action. This energy of anger can be used to combat the forces of evil and to heal the consequences.

William Booth, founder of the Salvation Army, worked day and night among social outcasts in the worst urban conditions in the history of the Western world—the slums of nineteenth-century London. He prayerfully preached, cared, campaigned, organized, inspired, innovated, recruited, and administered for sixteen to eighteen hours a day for more than fifty years. Why? Because he was indignant about the moral, personal, and economic impoverishment of these members of God's family.

Anger directed at the evil of disease activated Dr. Tom Dooley to remain in the steaming jungle laboring to bring health to others even as his own health drained away. It seems to me that Christian activists like these have been physically propelled, at least in part, by energy arising from their anger with evil.

Out of Our Apathy

The activation set off by anger prods us out of our apathy. It helps us push aside our fears and jump into the fight against the pain of evil. While it is true that angry feelings can quickly lead to destructive behavior, this hazard can be overcome. More Christians are hurt by underinvolvement than by excessive intensity in living.

These are beneficial effects of the actual feeling of anger. There are also benefits from constructively handling angry feelings. The fact is, first, that anger is better than the alternatives. We have ruled out rage and also noted that to deny oneself the expression of anger is destructive. It is difficult, if not impossible, for us to have reasonable self-esteem if we are doing harmful things to others, and it is impossible for us to be fully effective in God's service if we are wounding ourselves. So we resolve anger or express it appropriately, depending on the circumstances. Both reap benefits.

Anger can be the first step toward understanding, caring and sharing, and mutual respect between persons. Maybe we have had a smoldering anger toward each other for a long time but we selfishly have put off working out the situation. When our resentment flares up, the heat of conflict may push us to solve our problems. It's not the ideal way, because of the risk, but good can come from it.

Relationships become more meaningful and honest when they are allowed the full range of emotional expression. I am talking about the appropriate expression of anger and resentment, and I certainly am not advocating any form of ranting and raving as an ordinary social activity.

Persons who express anger appropriately are treated with more respect than those who don't. They are seen as being honest, alive, and energetic. People who refuse to express their anger openly are viewed with disdain because of their lack of confidence and low self-esteem. On the other hand, as we express anger, *respect* for us goes up, but *affection* for us may go down—especially if the friendship has been built on the other person taking advantage of us.

Leads to Creativity

Second, anger can lead to creativity. Pounding ourselves against the brick wall of frustration can frazzle us to shreds and lead to anger. But if necessity is the mother of invention, frustration is the mother of creativity. Determination, persistence, and creativity should develop in us during periods of frustration as we use them to seek solutions to problems. These will develop if we want them to—it is our choice.

It worked this way for a minor-league hockey player. A National Hockey League club had promised him a trip to its tryout camp, but then reneged. According to newspaper reports, "That lit a fire under him." The player said, "This has generated a madness inside me to go out and prove that I belong in the NHL." With his increased determination, he cut his penalty time in half, more than doubled his goals, and earned a contract with a top NHL club.

His anger did not get him to the NHL—rather, it was his determination and hard work day after day that paid off. Yet the feeling of anger was there. He first avoided destroying himself with rage or resentment and then went the essential step further to channel the energy of anger into fierce determination to reach his goal. I do not advocate creating anger so that we can get activated, but when it is in us already, we ought to use it to help ourselves.

Finally, anger expressed in indignation benefits us because it is an expression of love. It is a reaction to evil. Uncomfortable and dangerous feelings of anger can be transformed into acts of caring. This can be beneficial to us and to others.

It is wrong for us not to express our indignation about an injustice if we are in a position to reduce or relieve that problem. This is true even if the effect of our indignation is but a ripple on the sea of injustice. It is our responsibility to both the victim and the perpetrator. While our obligation changes us, it increases our confidence and self-esteem.

The Benefits of Anger

Freeing Energy

The proper expression of our anger releases tension and frees energy for constructive activities that might otherwise be spent in suppressing anger. It avoids the wounds and barriers that are created by displaced or inappropriately expressed anger. So there is a great economy when anger is handled properly the first time around.

These are the benefits of the proper expression of anger. Rage and resentment, the destructive styles of handling anger, may also seem to have some benefits. These are illusions, however, because they work only briefly, and the side effects more than cancel out the benefits.

For example, rage can be used as a defensive strategy, a means of keeping people away. This affords some protection against being hurt by others, but denies the individual the acceptance and love that is needed. Rage is also a way of getting attention—another legitimate need—but the kind of attention we get this way does not provide acceptance. Negative attention can be better than being totally ignored, but it's not good enough.

A display of rage may relieve boredom, but it does so at the price of alienating others. Rage can be a way of retaliation, even when it is expressed only verbally. This may give us an evil sense of satisfaction, but in return we receive resentment and mistrust from others, fear of counterattack, and possibly feelings of guilt. Rage may also provide a release from frustration, but this feeling is not very satisfactory, because it is only the temporary absence of pain. Evidence is beginning to accumulate that this cathartic release can move into a self-perpetuating cycle of frustration—release through rage, temporary good feelings, and then frustration building once again.

Other Illusions

Resentment may also seem to have some benefits, but these likewise are illusions. Stifling our anger seems to be safer than dealing honestly with another person, and indeed in the short term it may be. It certainly can be easier than thinking through and preparing for a controversial discussion. Resentment is safe and easy, but ineffective because it doesn't improve things. We justify this by calling it "turning the other cheek" or by saying it denotes an easy-going, congenial person. This is actually lazy and selfish. If we let other people continue to do wrong by taking advantage of us, we have wronged them by failing to confront them. If we are silent in the face of injustice, we share the guilt. Resentment is not an easy way out, because of the self-destructive effect that is sure to result.

As Christians we are often so afraid of the hazards of anger that we fail to receive the benefits. We need to understand how to obtain the benefits of indignation while avoiding rage and resentment. If we are ready, responding to our angry feelings can lead to spiritual growth and effective Christian service. For this to happen, we need to know how to recognize the conditions for which indignation is the proper response and then learn how to express it in appropriate behavior.

15

Indignation: What, When, and How

We have described four kinds of responses to the feelings of anger: rage, resentment, resolution, and indignation. The first two are destructive: rage blows up the bridges people need to reach each other, and resentment sends people scurrying behind barriers to hide from each other and to hurt each other indirectly. Indignation is constructive: it seeks to heal hurts and to bring people together. Its purpose is to rebuild the bridges and pull down the barriers, yet it is like rage and resentment in that the feeling of anger remains.

It should be the most natural thing for a Christian to become angry over an injustice. We should be stirred with outrage at evil in whatever form it comes— disease, a racist's bomb, immorality, rocketing inflation, an outrageous price for a repair job, famine, a group of Christians squandering their energy in bickering or self-praise, corrupt government leadership, public indifference to crime, or any of a million other conditions.

But we should move beyond the feeling of anger into action to protest the evil and to do what we can to relieve human suffering. Indignation is the Christian's proper response to evil; it involves responding to the feeling of anger with a rationally selected, deliberate course of behavior designed to stop evil or relieve its effects.

At the first spark of anger, we must begin to decide what we will do. We have the choice of destructive rage or resentment; resolution with possible relief of the feeling; or indignation, in which the feeling of anger remains to provoke us to action.

Indignation can look a lot like rage, and there is nothing wrong with this per se. We have sometimes made loudness or softness of voice a clue to the morality of the anger. But note this: The behavior of Jesus when He drove the moneychangers out of the temple must have looked a lot like rage; but His motivation was healing, not revenge; help, not hurt. His behavior was other-serving, not self-serving. That is what counts.

Contrasting Motivations

As I was writing this book I often thought of the cliché used of anger, "veins popping out on the neck." I recall two instances in my life when I was aware of actually seeing this happen in a person who was angry with me. The physical and emotional intensity of the persons was similar in these cases, but their motivations were quite different.

The first situation occurred when, as a college student, I was called before a disciplinary committee and accused of a prank I did not commit. In fact, until I was accused, I had not even heard about the prank. One member of the committee didn't believe me. The little white-haired professor leaned forward, enough to rise off his chair, and—red-faced, veins protruding, and quivering with anger—shook his finger at me and shouted, "You did it! Admit it!"

On another occasion, a different professor sought me out in my dormitory room late at night and, with similar fervor, demanded that I immediately return the black and yellow barricade with amber flashing light that I had brought into the dormitory from a construction site. I sat on the edge of my bed as—red-faced, veins protruding, and quivering with anger—he towered over me while I tried to fake innocence and nonchalantly pointed out that it did "sort of brighten up the place."

"Take it back!" he shouted.

"I'll do it first thing tomorrow," I replied calmly.

"You'll do it tonight!"

"It's raining out there!"

"You'll do it tonight!"

"It's almost midnight!"

"You'll do it tonight!"

So I did. As I drove ten miles through the pounding rain and darkness to replace the barricade, I cried from guilt and shame. Now I feel gratitude for that man whose commitment to being my friend was so strong that he felt and expressed anger about my foolish behavior.

The first man wanted revenge to assuage his punctured conceit, and he let his anger lead him to rage. The second man wanted me to grow in maturity and self-respect so he channeled his anger into constructive, vigorous confrontation—loving indignation. Like Jesus, he showed that compassion could get "tough."

Charateristics of Indignation

Indignation is not distinguised from rage or resentment by the way it looks or feels, but rather by the attitudes and purposes from which it springs. Let us look at the characteristics of the appropriately indignant person.

The indignant person focuses on real injustice to self or others. The injustice is not imaginary; it can be identified, defined, measured, and verified by other persons.

The indignant person is realistic. Behavior is directed to where injustice can be reduced or its consequences relieved. We should not invest ourselves in indignant behavior if we cannot do *any* good, because there is an emotional and physical cost. In chasing the moneychangers from the temple, Jesus didn't start something He couldn't finish. The change wasn't permanent, but it was enough; He did what was His to do at that time. We may not be able to do enough, but we can do something.

The indignant person is unselfish. The fury of Jesus' indignant outburst to the Pharisees recorded in Matthew 23 centered on their failure to show justice, mercy, and faithfulness in their lives. When He confronted the Pharisees about this, Jesus showed justice, mercy, and faithfulness to those to whom the Pharisees had been unjust, cruel, and indifferent. He was a willing advocate of the mistreated, and He knew what price He would pay for His effort.

The indignant person is loving. In the incident at the synagogue when Jesus healed a man with a shriveled hand, Mark describes how Jesus looked at the Pharisees in anger even while being "deeply distressed at their stubborn hearts" (Mark 3:5). He felt angry over the hypocrisy of the Pharisees and angry about their efforts to keep people from the truth about God, but He loved the Pharisees anyway. He wanted them, too, to receive healing in their lives. Yet He knew they wouldn't, and it distressed Him. Only love is distressed to see enemies hurt themselves.

The indignant person stays under control. When Jesus cleared the temple, He acted within the range of His authority, and His behavior did not violate His principles. True, the full measure of His authority was not understood even by His disciples, and the incident fueled the opposition of the religious leaders. But He knew what He was doing, and His behavior was righteous. We should test our behavior against scriptural principles and, if at all possible, consult with other believers to make sure our actions are acceptable and sensible.

The indignant person keeps his life in balance. Our indignant behavior should not destroy our effectiveness in another part of life. For example, I can think of a man who is so dedicated to opposing drug abuse that he has neglected his relationship with his own children. His desire to fight immorality is fine; but letting this become so important that it injures his own children is deplorable and inexcusable. The indignant Christian monitors his or her life to keep activities in balance.

Proactive Lifestyle

To live up to this set of characteristics seems like a pretty tall order. It is. It has to be, because indignation combines the intensity of rage with purity of purpose, and that isn't easy.

How do we manage this? First, expressing indignation needs to be done within the context of a proactive lifestyle. The term *proactive lifestyle* refers to living vigorously centered on God's patterns. Proactive people refuse to accept passively whatever comes or to be controlled by circumstances, and they also refuse to be controlled by their emotions, reacting selfishly, violently, or carnally. Proactive people seek to follow God's commands to be holy. They seek to be God's servants, and the servants of others despite opposition or a price to pay. The proactive person energetically seeks to build a lifestyle founded on the principles mentioned above.

When we consider indignation, we look at just one of many facets of proactive living. It is a particularly strategic one, however, because it has often been misunderstood.

Indignant protest is needed. But not enough is given. And that which is given is rarely received, often because it is offered in the wrong way. Therefore we need to learn to protest effectively. Perhaps we need to organize a "ministry of indignation," for without effective protest, offenses continue, offenders multiply, and perhaps worse of all, victims multiply. Let us look at some specific suggestions about how to express indignation effectively.

We should pray within ourselves as we express indignation.

144

Indignation: What, When, and How

Before expressing our indignation we may have the opportunity to write out our feelings and what we might say to another person. We probably won't use the actual paper, but the preparation will help us. If we can, we should go over our words with another person.

We must forgive. The importance of this is covered in chapter 9. Separating the person and his or her action is important. What do we gripe about? People usually say: "Well, the mayor made another one of his stupid blunders." "This guy at work is so stupid!" "The church will never grow as long as you people are so . . ." It's okay to dislike the offensive behavior, but we are commanded to love the person who expresses it. When we talk with that person, we should talk about the bad behavior, rather than assulting their dignity.

Attacking the Problem

For example, we can say, "You left my bicycle out in the rain. It has an expensive leather seat, and the rain ruined it. I'm pretty disappointed in your carelessness and upset about the damage that has been done."

This contrasts with attacking the person, saying, "What's the matter with you? Anyone with a brain and any sense of responsibility would not leave a bike in the rain! You probably don't have enough sense to come in out of the rain yourself!" That's rage, not indignation; it attacks the person, not the problem. Refuse to let yourself indulge in name-calling and sarcasm.

Reporting what has happened rather than blaming someone for it may help relieve our strongest tensions about the situation. Blaming is not productive. It provokes aggression in the other person. The approach of reporting gives the other person the opportunity to accept responsibility if he or she is ready to. If the other verson is not ready to take responsibility, the other things we might do probably wouldn't work anyway.

We should channel our energy constructively toward correcting the damage, but we should also give the other person a chance to take his or her share of responsibility. For example, we could ask, "The bike seat needs repair. Would you mind rubbing leather conditioner into it?"

Threats usually do not work in a relationship. Although they have a place, they are risky, because they incite rebellion and we may not be able to back them up. They are more of a last resort than a routine method.

We must be honest. What we say must spring directly out of our true strong beliefs and must not be dramatic just to make a point. Selfishness or other sins can easily contaminate indignation.

These are a few main points in the process. Of greatest importance is that we be available to be used in the Lord's service and that we learn through His on-the-job-training process. The following prayer states what our attitude toward sin should be and our readiness to combat it:

I'm Ready for Assignment, Lord

You have settled me, Lord.

My life was a corn popper, the fragments of my will leaping frantically, exploding in a frenzy of activity that only confused me.

You entered with love—reassuring, soothing, comforting. I have learned to trust you, to lean on you, and even to jump for joy with trampoline enthusiasm once in a while in confident celebration of your love.

Indignation: What, When, and How

You have planted some of that love in me. Nurture it, please, until it is strong enough that I am willing to learn to care about others. Lead me out of the closet of my selfishness and into the coliseum of service.

Unsettle me, Lord.

Give me the gift of discomfort at the brokenness of my world. Teach me to be sensitive enough to agonize when I see the agony of my brothers and sisters. Let me see injustice and other sin vividly enough so that I will never tolerate it.

Give me a vision of helping. Develop in me determination to be a mender of brokenness. Help me to learn what I can do. If you wish, give me a ministry of indignation: to be one who complains, clamors, or nags in protest against the brutality of sin.

Keep me going—to face hard tasks when they appear and to care when I am tired of caring. Let me have the aliveness of the corn popper—the heat and the noise, even—but replace the helter-skelter with a clear direction of purpose. May I depend on you so that it is your unlimited power working through me and not just my flimsy efforts.

And may you receive all praise and glory, for ever and ever!

16

Let's Get On With Living

A speck of grit in our eye can make us want to scream. One tiny particle so small that a thousand of them wouldn't add up to the size of a little fingernail can become the force that controls our lives at that moment. Yet it is only one fragment of all the many forces in our lives.

Anger is like that. It is just a fragment of the whole, but if we let it, it can grow until it becomes the force that controls the rest of our lives.

We have explored anger in many dimensions. There is some danger in magnifying one little piece of life in such detail, because we don't live that way. In reality, any specific part of life, such as anger, is intermingled with many other feelings, attitudes, and beliefs. All these grow from our life experience and self-image, are in the context of relationships with other persons and with God, and appear amid the varied things we do.

But we live in an age of rage, so it has been useful to pay particular attention to this emotion. By studying anger and its power, we can learn self-control so that we do not need to *lose* our temper in rage or *abuse* ourselves with resentment, but can *defuse* anger by resolving circumstances and then *use* the energy of anger through Christlike indignation.

The following summary, written in the form of resolutions, can form a point of departure for us as we continue with life. We should reflect prayerfully about how we can incorporate these ideals in our own lives.

—To keep my life centered on God, as best I can, recognizing that when I do not, my natural self will generate things to become angry about;

—To not condemn myself for feelings of anger;

—To do everything I can to avoid acting on the basis of anger;

—To clean up any problems I create as quickly as possible;

—To recognize God's help in this process;

—To redirect the energy of anger away from hurting people and toward improving conditions for people;

—To be sensitive to injustice and evil, learning to be angry about the misery that sin inflicts on people without becoming controlled by the anger.

It has been my observation, in counseling on problems of anger control, that each person who has sought God's help in the understanding and resolution of his or her anger has, without exception, received that help. These people have often described the results as "miraculous." There is, indeed, a miracle involved. It is the miracle of God's love for us, the miracle of His redemptive grace.

Most importantly, it is first of all our relationship with God that ultimately matters. He has given us principles to follow, and the skills and techniques presented here are compatible with those principles. Although these skills and techniques are useful for anyone, it is our relationship with Him that makes it possible for us to use them properly to live in harmony with His principles.

Since our relationship with God is of greatest importance, let us keep our attention centered there. Part of His creation is the emotion of anger. Let us offer that part of our selves to Him along with every other part.

The Prayer of an Angry Person

Loving God, I praise You for Your wisdom, for Your love, for Your power. Thank You for life, with its joys and mysteries. Thank You for emotions—including anger.

Forgive me when I am led by my anger instead of being led by You. Make me aware of the things I do that produce anger in others—help me change those things. Show me how to clean up the offenses I commit toward others, and give me the courage to ask forgiveness.

Help me to be able to look past the anger of another person and see Your creation in them, and to love them. Teach me how to forgive; and give me the humility to forgive gracefully.

Arouse me to oppose injustice and other evils. Show me how to channel my energy that might otherwise be wasted in anger into constructive action in Your service.

You ask me to minister to persons around me. Help me understand what that means. Wake me up. Help me recognize that every moment of my life is an opportunity for Your love to flow through me.

Thank You, heavenly Father, for Your love. Thank You

for sending Christ so that we might have life and have it to the full, and for sending the Holy Spirit to comfort and guide us through the uncertainties and confusion of everyday living.

In Christ's name, Amen.

17

Personal Action Plans

The purpose of this book is to help us improve the quality of our lives. The logical conclusion to this discussion is to apply some action plans as presented in this chapter. They supplement the activities in other chapters and will help us put the principles of the book into practice so that we will benefit from the feeling of anger and not be hurt by it.

We may not find all the sections of equal value, but we should read the entire chapter and identify what applies personally, then prayerfully work on it.

Section A. Am I Angry?

1. Here is a list of active behaviors that are usually signs of anger. Honestly evaluate whether any of these characterize you, even mildly, and identify the target person:

Sarcasm	Bullying
Teasing	Intolerance
Cruelty	Overcompetitiveness
Argumentativeness	

2. Here are some passive behaviors that occur generally in the privacy of our own minds or outside the awareness of other persons. Consider whether you associate any of these behaviors with specific people:

Self-pity	Unforgiving spirit	Stubbornness
Restlessness	Fearfulness	Pride
Nervousness	Depression	Illness
Selfishness	Self-righteousness	Withdrawal

Section B. What Am I Angry About?

Think through all the dimensions of your life. The list of areas below will help you organize your thoughts. Add any other aspects that you think of. As you read through this list, jot down the first three things that come to mind in each category, whether or not those thoughts seem to have any anger component in them. You will be identifying at least thirty-six things that are at the forefront of your consciousness. These will be matters that are important to you. When you get angry, it concerns something that is important to you, so this form of free association can help you pinpoint some of your feelings and their sources.

Leisure time/hobbies/fun	National conditions
Family	World conditions
Job/school	God
Church	Friends
Neighborhood	Your future life
Your life in the past	Your physical health

Section C. Do I Need to Apologize?

List the ten people with whom you spend the most time. Prayerfully reflect whether you have committed any offense toward them for which you should apologize. Write this down, and set a deadline date by which you will have apologized for it and determined whether there should be restitution.

Section D. Do I Resolve It or Stay Indignant?

We confront a crucial question each time we feel angry. Here are some guidelines that, in addition to those in chapter 5, can help you make that decision. Do not stay angry unless you can give positive answers to these guidelines.

1. There is an actual, identifiable injustice or wrong being done to someone.

2. Scripture supports my point of view about that.

3. I have consulted another person and he or she agrees.

4. I can do something about this injustice. I have time, I can handle it without losing control of my feelings, and it will not be a drain on other responsibilities I have.

5. There is evidence of love in other parts of my life. This is important, because Christ hated wickedness but loved right (Heb. 1:9). If we do not have evidence that we too love right, we are on very dangerous ground as we begin to start hating and acting against wickedness.

6. This action will benefit another person. I am not doing this as a "glory trip."

7. I have all the facts that I can obtain.

Personal Action Plans

Section E. Checklist of "First Aid" Strategies

For review, here is a list of the "first aid" strategies presented in chapter 7. Check those that have been most beneficial to you. Add others to the list.

Asking for God's help
1. Recognize that God is in control.
2. Pray with thanksgiving and praise.
3. Pray for peace in your heart.
4. Think or read Scripture.
5. Pray for the person.

Human willful control
6. Measure the issue.
7. Control yourself.
8. Remind yourself that an angry feeling is okay.
9. Divert your attention.
10. Separate yourself from the conflict.
11. Change to a different scene.
12. Maintain positive thoughts.
13. Use music.
14. Channel the energy.
15. Do something you enjoy.
16. Talk with a friend.
17. Talk with yourself.
18. Laugh.
19. Cry.
20. Write it down.
21. Relax.

Section F. Who Do I Need to Forgive?

1. Use your list of ten people from section C. Examine that list again to see whether you can identify persons you need to forgive.

2. Here is a summary checklist of the steps in the forgiving process described in chapter 9.

    a. Decide that you are willing to want to forgive.

    b. Begin to want to forgive.

    c. Quit hurting the other person.

    d. Rehearse the act of forgiving.

    e. Arrange a time to talk with the other person.

    f. Be gracious in your conversation.

    g. Make an explicit statement of forgiveness.

    h. Listen, no matter what.

    i. Explain why you wanted to talk about this.

    j. Claim the closing of this incident.

For each person whom you need to forgive, mark what parts of the process have been fulfilled. Set goals for the remaining tasks.

Section G. Improving My Attitude
Toward a Person With Whom I Am Angry

One of the big barriers to resolving anger with another person is that we often don't understand him or her well enough. Perhaps we actually have the facts we need, but we haven't allowed those facts to break through and affect our attitudes. Here are two simple procedures that will help you use your knowledge about another person to develop a better attitude toward him or her.

1. List all the positive things you can think of about this person.

2. List the sources of stress in this person's life. What hardships is he or she dealing with? What disappointments? What frustrations? Thinking with empathy in this way helps greatly to soften our feelings of hostility.

Section H. Checklist of "Cure" Strategies

For quick reference, here is a list of the "cure" strategies from chapter 8. Check those that have been helpful to you, and add others to the list. What do you need to do now to resolve a particular conflict? When are you going to do it? Make a specific plan.

1. Learn to be aware of anger.
2. Undo any damage.
3. Ask God for help.
4. Decide what your response should be—resolution or indignation.
5. Don't keep anger going.
6. Bring the problem into perspective.
7. Find and analyze the sources of anger.
8. Vocally renounce the inappropriate options.
9. Plan your constructive actions.
    a. Tell the other person.
    b. Confront.
    c. Conduct a group pow-wow.
    d. Forgive.
    e. Ask for the other person's help.
    f. Develop friendship.
10. Visualize and rehearse the resolution of anger.

Section I. Life Goals

If you feel you could be at a better place in life, you ought to get there as soon as you can. Goals help. Without specific goals, our path of improvement will be zigzag, a personal "wandering in the wilderness," and we probably won't get where we want to go.

Set some goals and write them down. A goal should be attainable with difficulty. The best goals stretch our personal abilities and push us into greater dependence on the Lord. A goal should be stated in a way so it can be measured. For example, the statement "To be a better person" can't be measured. A goal stated "To attend every session of my Bible study group unless I am sick" can be measured. The goal should be scriptural, which means it will be moral and worthwhile.

Think about the internal conditious—guilt, sense of helplessness, unrealistic expectations, and aimlessness—and the external conditions—loss, threat, frustration, and rejection—discussed in chapter 4. Study these one at a time and write down ways you would like conditions to be different in your life in regard to each. These are goals. What are you going to do about them? These are plans for reaching the goals. For each goal and plan, set a date by which you will either accomplish it or review it. One of the advantages of writing down goals is that we can rejoice about the progress that we have made.

Section J. Checklist of Prevention Strategies

This is a summary of the strategies in chapter 11. Check those that are most applicable to you. Add others to the list. At present, what is your most vulnerable situation? What is your plan for dealing with it?

1. Clean up the old mess.
   a. Evaluate your internal conditions.
   b. Practice proactive living.
2. Become a stronger, more mature Christian.
   a. Develop spiritual strength.
   b. Look at the person, not at the behavior.
   c. Be interested in other persons.
   d. Have flexibility with others.

   e. Keep open communications.

   f. See the other person's point of view.

3. Evaluate your life.

   a. Understand how pressure builds in you.

   b. When you feel anger coming, review what you know about anger.

   c. Do not let your emotional system get overloaded.

   d. Stay in good physical shape.

   e. Walk around trouble.

   f. Be prepared.

   g. Develop your sense of humor.

   h. Cultivate optimism.

   i. Change habits when this is needed.

Section K. Anger Toward God

Review in your mind and in prayer your relationship with God. Is there unfinished business with Him? Old grudges? Secret anger you tried to hide from Him?

Use the same process to clear up the defects in your relationship with God that you would use with another person. There is this one marvelous difference: With God there is no risk. No matter what sinful feelings we have allowed to lurk in the recesses of our hearts, God forgives us and loves us totally. Honor Him by confessing anything you need to confess, and discover the completeness of His love for you.

Section L. Indignation

1. List injustices and suffering in several categories:

World affairs (e.g., famine, political oppression)
Your country (e.g., racial discrimination, unequal opportunities for adequate housing)

159

The church (e.g., bickering, apathy)
Your place of work (e.g., favoritism in applying policies, unethical practices)

List as many things as you can, whether or not a particular problem gets you stirred up. From the list, check those about which you have the strongest feelings. Consider whether you can make the world a better place by contributing your small part to speak out or to act against these individual or corporate sins. What can you do?

2. Write a letter expressing your indignation about any one of these. The letter might be to people in charge (a corporate president or a politician) or to a newspaper. Go on record with your view. Your public library can help you find addresses.

3. Pray daily for thirty days using the prayer "I'm Ready for Assignment, Lord" or a similar prayer in your own words. Seek the service tasks that are right for you, and ask for courage and wisdom to embark on these tasks in service to our Lord.

4. What if it seems as though it was the other person's action that made you indignant? It may be that your anger is a natural response to being abused. Read Matthew 18:15–17. Have you ever been sinned against by a Christian brother? What has been your response? Has that response been the best one? Is there any situation like this active in your life now? What are you going to do about it?